Library

D0102326

Exploring Woodland

The Lake District & The Northwest

101 beautiful woods to visit

078229

0 7 8 2 2 9

Collins is an imprint of HarperCollins*Publishers* Ltd.
77–85 Fulham Palace Road
London
W6 8JB

The Collins website address is: www. collins.co.uk

10 09 08 07 06 05 04

10 9 8 7 6 5 4 3 2 1

ISBN 0 00 717548 5

First published in 2004
Text © The Woodland Trust 2004
Maps © HarperCollins*Publishers* except p22 and p54 © The Woodland Trust

The authors assert their moral right to be identified as the authors of this work. All rights reserved. The Author and Publishers of this book have made every effort to ensure that the information contained in this book is accurate and as up-to-date as possible at the date of publication. Any reliance upon the accuracy of the information contained in this book is entirely at the reader's own risk. Woodland sites and the countryside in general are likely to change and develop over time as a result of both man and nature. Care should be taken at all times when in the countryside and readers are advised especially to read and follow any safety instructions or notices and keep to public footpaths wherever possible.

The copyright in the photographs belongs to the following:
Woodland Trust Picture Library: 14, 15, 22, 24, 38, 42, 47, 65, 75, 81; Stuart Handley 4, 6, 8, 9, 10, 11, 12, 13, 48, 51, 53, 62, 63, 66, 70, 76, 77, 78, 82, 85, 86, 87; Archie Miles 7 (top), 16, 28, 30, 32, 44; English Nature 20; National Trust Picture Library: Mike Williams 9 (bottom), Joe Cornish 60, Matthew Antrobus 69, Geoff Morgan 89; Forest Life Picture Library/Forestry Commission 27; Val Corbett 36, 37; Ingleton Scenery Company 54; Burnley Borough Council 56; Croxteth Country Park 72

A catalogue record for this book is available from the British Library.

Site maps produced by Belvoir Cartographics and Design
Designed by Liz Bourne
Site entries written by Sheila Ashton, researched by Diana Moss
Edited by Graham Blight

Printed and bound by Printing Express Ltd., Hong Kong
All the paper used in this book is 100% recycled

HOW TO USE THIS BOOK

Covering a region that encompasses the Lake District and Northwest England, this book is divided into three areas represented by key maps on pp18–19, 40–41 and 58–59. The tree symbols on these maps denote the location of each wood. In the pages following the key maps, the sites nearest one another are described together (wherever practical) to make planning a day out as rewarding as possible.

For each site entry the name of the nearest town/village is given, followed by road directions and the grid reference of the site entrance. The area of the site (in hectares (HA) followed by acres) is given next together with the official status of the site where appropriate. The owner, body or organisation responsible for maintaining the site is given next. Symbols are used to denote information about the site and its facilities. These are explained on p17.

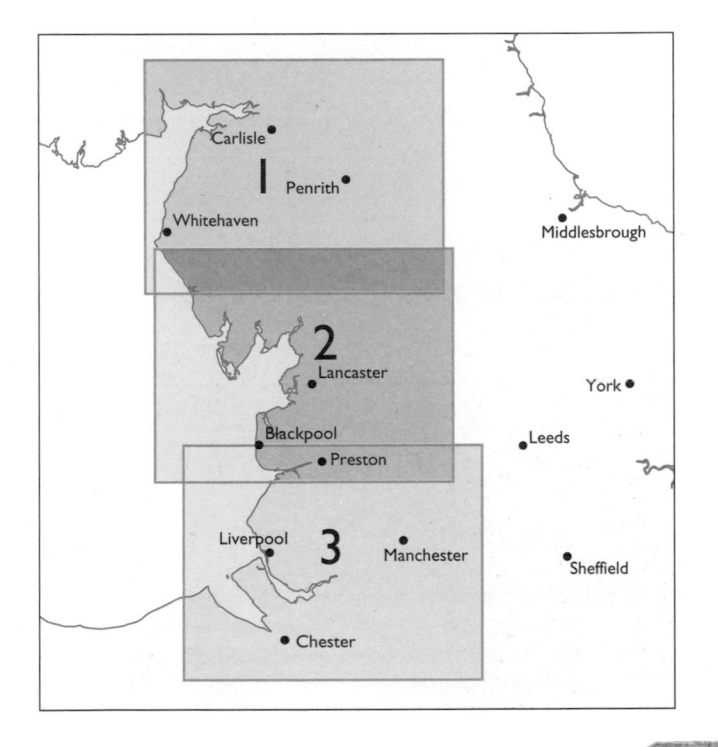

INTRODUCTION

Woodland Trust celebrity supporter, Alistair McGowan, says:
'Can you imagine what our countryside would look like without
trees? Sound like a colourless and dreary place? Woods offer us
peace and tranquillity, inspire our imagination and creativity, and
refresh our souls. A land without trees would be a barren, cold
and impoverished place. When I want to get back in touch with
nature and escape from the hustle and bustle of my daily life, I
love to visit and explore these natural treasures. These places are
rich in wildlife and support a wide variety of animal and plant life.
This excellent series of Woodland Trust guidebooks charts some
of the most spectacular woods across the UK. You will be amazed
and inspired to discover the wide variety of cultural and ecological
history that exists in these special places. Each guide provides you
with the all the information you will ever need.'

THE LAKES & THE NORTHWEST

Cast a glance at the maps of the northwest region covered within this guide and the first impression is a land of stark contrasts. To the south any woodland sites appear to vie for space with the intensive network of motorways, roads and merging settlements of the Manchester and Liverpool conurbations. Whilst 60 miles to the north that ever popular tourism honey pot, The Lake District, its dramatic vistas the inspiration for generations of poets and artists, has room for great tracts of woodland, some well frequented and others more remote and less familiar.

It is widely appreciated today that trees, parks and woodland are the green lungs of the urban environment. We all need green oases to refresh the body and soul, and fortunately it would seem that our forebears felt much the same, particularly those with the wherewithal to make a difference.

Many of the south Lancashire woodlands featured within were either created or bolstered by the endeavours of wealthy local landowners with a desire to acquire their very own designer tracts of countryside; often to provide cover for their game or to supply the timber and fuel needs of their estates and businesses. However, with increasing demands upon the land available throughout the last 200 years it seems a miracle that there is any woodland left at all, but the Victorians were well aware that sustainability was the watchword for woodland management. As with so many parts of Britain in close proximity to industry a strict coppice regime was the only way to ensure that the wood, charcoal and tan bark to keep mill, foundry and factory in full spate was readily available.

Wood sorrel in Dufton Ghyll, p24

Extensively planted or managed woodlands once linked to estates survive in several different forms, depending upon the predilections of their owners, and may often still contain introduced or exotic species. One of the biggest mistakes these landowners did make though was their fascination with the newly arrived rhododendron. At first a showy and successful shrub on the acidic soils, but currently viewed with some dismay as an ever spreading all suppressing weed.

Crab apple harvest,
Moss & Height Spring, p42

One of the most spectacular examples of these large estate schemes is Lever Park, set on the slopes of Rivington Pike, once the home of the great industrial philanthropist Lord Leverhulme. Here, a landscape comprised of broadleaf woodland, avenues, parkland and gardens has been carved from the rugged hillside. Daisy Nook (what a sweet name – surely fairies must live here) was part of the estate of the now ruinous Riversvale Hall and here it is still possible to trace remnants of an old arboretum amongst the naturally regenerating woodland. Raveden, near Bolton, is also a woodland once managed as an extension to the pleasure grounds of Smithills Hall; whilst Towneley Woods, near Burnley, reveals the indulgencies of the owners of Towneley Hall with once grand re-landscaping schemes of the 19th century complete with a splendid array of follies and grottoes. As a modern extension to this theme there is now a new generation of woodland sculptures appearing here and there along the walks.

Footbridge crossing stream in Northern Woods, Styal Estate, p84

Ferns and mossy boulders, Hyning, p51

Although the endeavours of the great and the good made a valuable contribution to Lancashire's tree cover in the past, today it needs the concerted efforts of government policy and grass roots enthusiasm to make radical woodland expansion possible. Over the last 15 years there have been 12 Community Forests slowly evolving throughout England, two of these being, The Red Rose Forest, in and around Greater Manchester, and The Mersey Forest (the largest), covering some 110,000 hectares (270,000 acres) of Merseyside and north Cheshire. A partnership between the Countryside Agency, the Forestry Commission, local authorities and many other local and national partners has provided a programme of woodland regeneration in urban areas, and with the involvement of people in the respective communities, a greener and more pleasant land for many city dwellers looks a distinct reality in the future.

As a county Lancashire is fairly sparsely wooded, and it seems likely that this has been the case for hundreds of years. Industry and

Stone wall edging, Gisburn Forest, p53

Small tortoiseshell on bracken, Warton Crag, p51

agriculture pushed back the woodland cover to the most inaccessible areas on the poorest land, such as the steep acidic valley sides known locally as cloughs. Here it was difficult to actively manage the woodland and virtually impregnable to marauding flocks of sheep. Tree cover here is often oak with birch in the upper reaches, with sycamore, ash and wych elm prevailing along the valley bottoms. Sycamore, much pilloried in other parts of Britain, is very successful and, as well as providing excellent timber, it manifests as a distinctive shelter tree in some of the more exposed locations. Traditionally the wood was prized by the bobbin makers who crafted millions of bobbins for the cotton and wool industries.

Before heading north it's well worth a coastal detour to take in a remarkable wood at Formby. This salt laden seaside wood predominantly of Scots pine (but also including some Maritime and Corsican pine) was planted in 1900 with the intention of stabilising the sand dunes and eventually to build a promenade. That never happened, but what did happen, and largely because of the island habitat created by the developed hinterland, was the ongoing survival of a colony of red squirrels. There may be no better place to observe these delightful little characters, and what's more they are bold enough to be fed by visitors.

The middle of Lancashire may appear somewhat misleading in its appellation as the Forest of Bowland, for it is not, as some would assume, a forest of dense tree cover, but now merely an administrative region containing scattered small woodlands. The word 'forest' has become inextricably linked in the minds of most people to regions dominated by trees and woodland, yet its true meaning harks back to the Norman Conquest, when William I established the first royal forests. These were exclusive preserves held by the crown principally for the purpose of hunting, although eventually economic reasons also prevailed. By the 13th century a quarter of the country was designated as royal forest, and it just so happened that the majority of these were in the wilder and more wooded parts. Travel to Scotland and there are forests where you

Lumb Brook Valley provides a peaceful oasis, p82

may ramble for days with barely a sight of a single tree!

However, on the northern tip of Lancashire, above Carnforth, lie the remarkable woodlands of Silverdale and Arnside, where carboniferous limestone dictates a rich diversity of vegetation. Gait Barrows (a National Nature Reserve) is one of the finest examples of limestone pavement in Britain with its associated woodland of stunted yew, ash, rowan, hazel and birch struggling improbably from the depths of the rocky grikes. Here and there a Scots pine, a juniper, a buckthorn or the locally specific *Sorbus lancastriensis*, one of the country's rarest whitebeams. Many of these trees, although relatively small, are probably extremely old; the arduous conditions creating natural semi-bonsai forms. The woods around the pavement areas contain the same mix of trees, but with rather more normal size and appearance. An astounding number of more than 1,600 types of fungi and 800 species of moths have been identified here, not to mention all the plants and butterflies too! It's one of those places you just have to revisit time and again. A short step away lies Eaves Wood. Yet again bands of limestone span the woodland floor, but here, unlike Gait Barrows, a little more shelter from the elements has allowed loam to collect amongst the rocky crevices, giving rise to some splendid yews and, in the site's lower hollows, truly beautiful old small-leaved lime coppice stools. These mossy old limes are almost certainly many hundreds of years old and occur very close to the tree's northern range limit. Due to colder climatic conditions this species no longer sets viable seed and so they represent the last of their line in northern Britain, only proliferating through coppicing or natural layering. A chock-a-block car park here reflects the wood's popularity, offering such features as a mature planted circle of tall beeches (with the usual adornments made by trysting lovers) and a tower folly called the Pepper Pot, with excellent views of Morecambe Bay.

Near the village of Arnside lies a 150 metre (500 foot) limestone hill known as Arnside Knott, again with fine views across the Bay to the distant Lake District. Named because of its now defunct knotted larch trees, conjoined in the 19th century as a love token (old postcards illustrating these may still be found), the Knott's close proximity to habitation rather creates the impression of a public park. Tree cover varies from dense oak with hazel, rowan, holly and some splendid yews around the slopes to the sparser vegetation of the heathland on the hill top and a number of craggy old pines.

Further north and a swing westward into the southern Lake District of Cumbria and one is revelling in the region known as The Furness. This has always been a well wooded part of the country and certainly this was ensured up until the early 20th century by the attentive management of local industries who depended upon the coppice wood for charcoal manufacture used for iron smelting and tan bark for the leather industry. Latterly much of the broadleaf cover gave way to the Forestry Commission's conifer plantations, but in most recent times the balance is once again tipping back in favour of more broadleaf woodland.

Gap in drystone wall, Warton Crag, p51

Tangle of exposed roots, Raveden Wood, p66

Typically most of Cumbria's ancient woodland is comprised of birch and sessile oak, but in the more verdant valley bottoms and hollows ash, wych elm and hazel are evident, and where limestone outcrops appear yews, often of great proportions or with gnarled and sprawling forms, imbue their woods with a sense of mystery and wonder.

Not all of Cumbria is as well endowed with woodland as The Furness for the traditional counterbalance to successful tree growth has historically been the presence of sheep. Coppice woodland was jealously guarded by those whose livelihoods depended upon it, and that wasn't just in relation to iron and leather. Coppice wood was crucial for pit props, furniture makers, coopers, cloggers, bobbin turners, basket makers; and larger timbers were always required for building houses and ships. Records

Rocky outcrops on Helsby Hill, p78

show, for example, that oak timbers from Sea Wood, at Bardsea, were floated from the wood's edge at high tide and towed round to the shipyards of nearby Ulverston. These woods still tumble down to the shoreline coping happily with the salt laden air, finishing a mere metre or two above the high tide-mark. The critical interdependence of all these woodland-based crafts and industries has now largely disappeared into the pages of history books, but a recent upsurge in interest from a dedicated band of contemporary craftsmen is seeing the resurrection of many virtually forgotten skills. This in turn puts a measure of vibrancy back into many of the long neglected coppice woods. Working woodland is healthy woodland!

The Forestry Commission has, since its inception, had a considerable presence in the Lake District. Largely as a result of a 1936 agreement between the Commission and the Council for the Preservation of Rural England, plantations of spruce, larch and Douglas fir have been restricted to the outlying areas of the region, allowing the survival of the ancient woodlands in most of the central Lake District. One extensive system which illustrates this rather well, although some limited planting has occurred in the more accessible tracts, is the Borrowdale Woods. A day or two spent exploring these remarkable woodlands provides a fascinating overview.

Southward from Keswick, Great Wood is the first encounter, with its striking zonal formation. On the shores of adjacent Derwent Water, water loving trees such as alder and willow predominate. A little way inland and towering stands of larch guard the lower fellsides, but as gentle slopes become craggy mountains the natural woodland of oak, ash, wych elm, birch, rowan, holly and hazel takes over, and in the upper reaches Scots pine also puts in an appearance. It is very quickly apparent that this wood, like the other Borrowdale woods, is richly endowed with wonderful colonies of mosses, lichens and liverworts, typically associated with Britain's Atlantic coast and its plentiful rainfall and pure air. Identifying some of the rarities in this field (which do occur here) will be lost on all but the experts, and yet close inspection of these tiny plants reveals an exquisite array of colour and form.

Moss and fern encrusted bank, Warton Crag p51

Lakeland views from Low Wood, p34

Along the valley, coach and car pull over so that visitors can take a brisk walk through Ashness Wood to visit the Bowder Stone, a mammoth glacial boulder carelessly left here by the glacier which shaped Borrowdale many millions of years ago. After marvelling at the size of this celebrity rock and taking a few photographs of it, on it and with it, most people file back to their cars, but Ashness Wood deserves further investigation, for it's a wonderful rocky undulating wood full of variety.

With Derwent Water behind, the tiny settlement of Seatoller is reached and hard by lies Johnny Wood. This is principally a woodland of oak coppice, most of which has now grown into tall spindly trees due to their close proximity. In the past grazing restricted growth of understorey trees and shrubs, yet now the woodland floor is a green boulder strewn carpet with a wealth of mosses and lichens.

Go that extra mile, to the end of Borrowdale, and close to the tiny settlement of Seathwaite seek out the Fraternal Four. These four impressive and ancient yew trees are found on the lower slopes of the western side of the valley, the largest having been nominated as one of Britain's Fifty Greatest Trees. However, it is recommended that you take your raincoat with you, since Seathwaite is officially the wettest inhabited place in England – receiving around 3,350mm (140 inches) of rain each year. Unbelievably, a September visit in 2002 found the River Derwent here as dry as a bone!

It is the water that shapes so many of the Lakeland woodlands, whether it be serene lakes, tumbling streams disgorging from mountain sides or babbling rivers meandering through broad valleys.

Gorse Covert Mounds, p83

To the west lies Eskdale, as good a place as any to enjoy water and woodland at one. The River Mite threads its way along the lower reaches of Miterdale Forest; birch, wild cherry and hazel sprouting from the water-logged banks, whilst on higher ground some fine stands of beech are found. Admittedly there is also a lot of forestry activity going on removing much of the softwood, but compartments of broadleaves remain and it is to be hoped that future regeneration and planting will be of this type. A good network of forest tracks makes this an ideal place for mountain biking or orienteering. An eerie experience here is to be alone in the wood and hear the distant mournful whistle of a steam train chugging along the nearby Ravenglass and Eskdale Railway.

For one of the most dramatic wet woodland experiences try the winding path up through Stanley Ghyll. Hugging the course of the stream from its relatively sedate lower reaches the path threads amongst larches and gigantic Douglas firs and soon climbs steeply through the narrowing gorge, criss-crossing the torrent by a series of bridges. Ever upward and the gorge becomes narrower and deeper,

the water more thunderous, the trees and ferns more tenuously anchored to the slippery sheer granite. It's hugely exhilarating to be perfectly safe (but watch your step on some of the wet paths) yet so close to the roar of danger.

Frankly, there's never a dull moment in the Lakeland woods, which may come as a surprise to many, since the star turns of the region have traditionally been the mountains

Snidley Moor, a local gem, p79

15

Sea Wood touches the shores of Morecambe Bay, p42

and lakes. With the fascinating vegetation, the dramatic terrain, the silvan vistas, and all the historic evidence of centuries of woodmanship seen in ancient coppice stools, old charcoal hearths and ancient trackways, there's plenty to enjoy.

Traversing the Lakeland uplands watch out for juniper – a strange little tree of the limestone which is our only native cypress. Easily mistaken for gorse bushes from a distance, juniper adopts a bizarre range of forms; from perfect, proper, tall and pointed specimens, akin to a fine Italian cypress, side by side with scruffy, weather-beaten, almost zoomorphic forms. Weather conditions such as persistent winds and heavy snows are the best explanation.

Weather has shaped many different exposed trees and it is often astounding to see how tenacious some Lakeland trees can be. One of the most dramatically successful species is the rowan, which appears to have the ability to thrive in the most exposed, barren and seemingly impossible locations. Trees often grow from tiny rock crevices in huge boulders or rock faces and there are many occurrences of quite large rowans growing within the forks of host trees of other species. How the root systems make it to terra firma or draw enough sustenance is a miracle.

Weird woodland experience of the year. The author, walking down Haverthwaite Heights, soaking up the early morning autumn sunshine, was suddenly brought up in his tracks as a peacock strutted haughtily across the path in front. You just never know for sure what's around the next woodland corner.

Archie Miles

Quick Reference

Symbols used to denote information about each site and the facilities to be found there.

Type of wood
☐ Mainly broadleaved woodland
☐ Mainly coniferous woodland
☐ Mixed woodland

Car Park
Ⓟ Parking on site
Ⓟ Parking nearby
Ⓟ Parking difficult to find

Status
AONB Area of Outstanding Natural Beauty
SSSI Site of Special Scientific Interest
NP National Park

Site Facilities
▨ Sign at entry
ⓘ Information board
♿ One or more paths suitable for wheelchair users
🐕 Dogs allowed under supervision
▨ Waymarked trail
🚻 Toilet
⛺ Picnic area
£ Entrance/car park charge
🍴 Refreshments on site

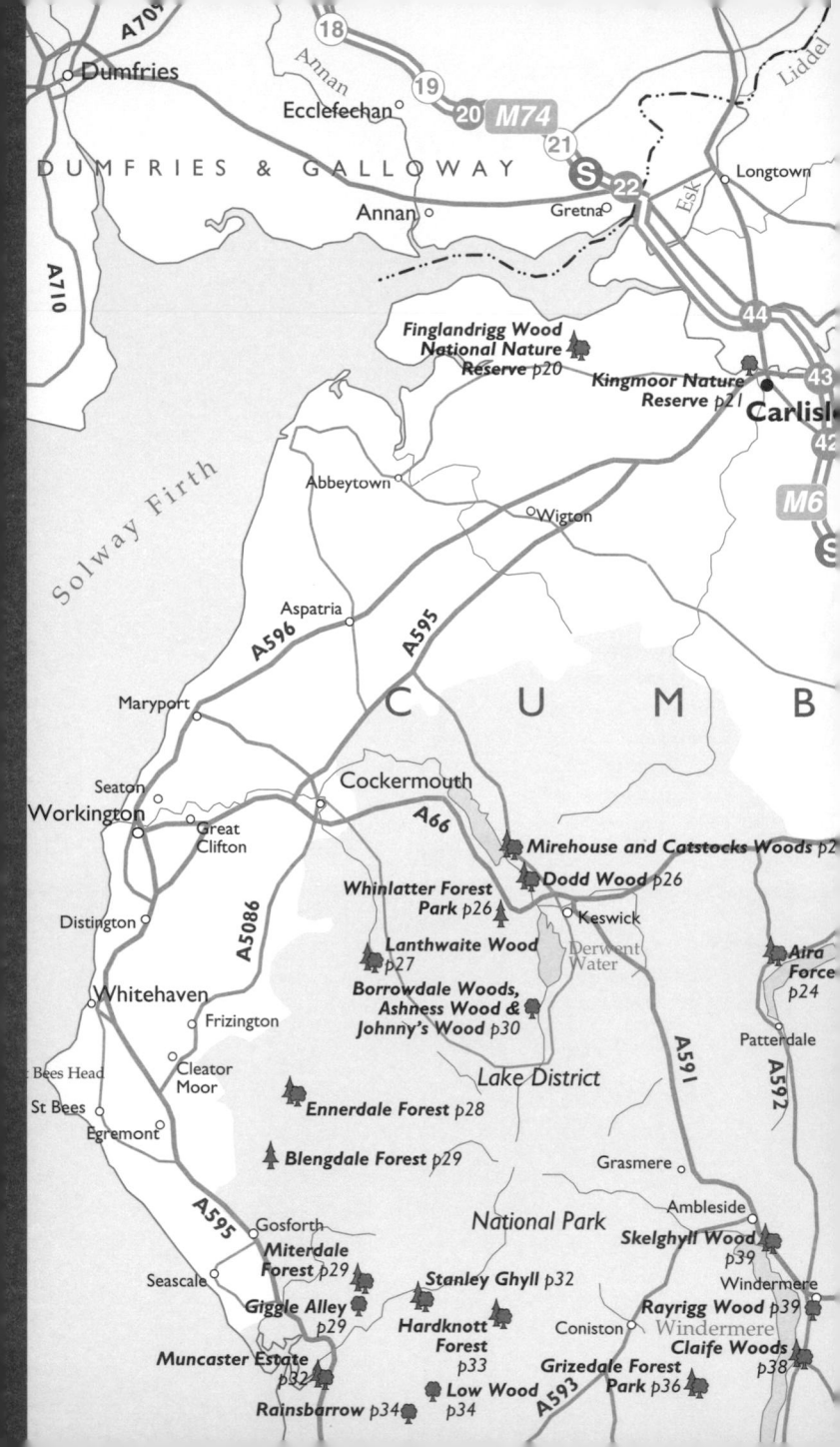

Dumfries

A709

A74

18

Annan

Ecclefechan

19

20 M74

21

DUMFRIES & GALLOWAY

S 22

Longtown

Annan

Gretna

Esk

Liddel

44

Finglandrigg Wood
National Nature
Reserve p20

Kingmoor Nature
Reserve p21

Carlisle

43

42

M6

Solway Firth

A710

Abbeytown

Wigton

S

Aspatria

A596

A595

C U M B

Maryport

Workington

Seaton

Great
Clifton

Cockermouth

A66

Mirehouse and Catstocks Woods p2

Dodd Wood p26

Distington

A5086

Whinlatter Forest
Park p26

Keswick

Whitehaven

Lanthwaite Wood
p27

Derwent
Water

Aira
Force
p24

Frizington

Borrowdale Woods,
Ashness Wood &
Johnny's Wood p30

Patterdale

Bees Head

Cleator
Moor

Lake District

A591

A592

St Bees

Ennerdale Forest p28

Egremont

Blengdale Forest p29

Grasmere

A595

Gosforth

National Park

Ambleside

Skelghyll Wood
p39

Miterdale
Forest p29

Stanley Ghyll p32

Windermere

Seascale

Rayrigg Wood p39

Giggle Alley
p29

Hardknott
Forest
p33

Coniston

Windermere

Claife Woods
p38

Muncaster Estate
p32

Grizedale Forest
Park p36

Rainsbarrow p34

Low Wood
p34

A593

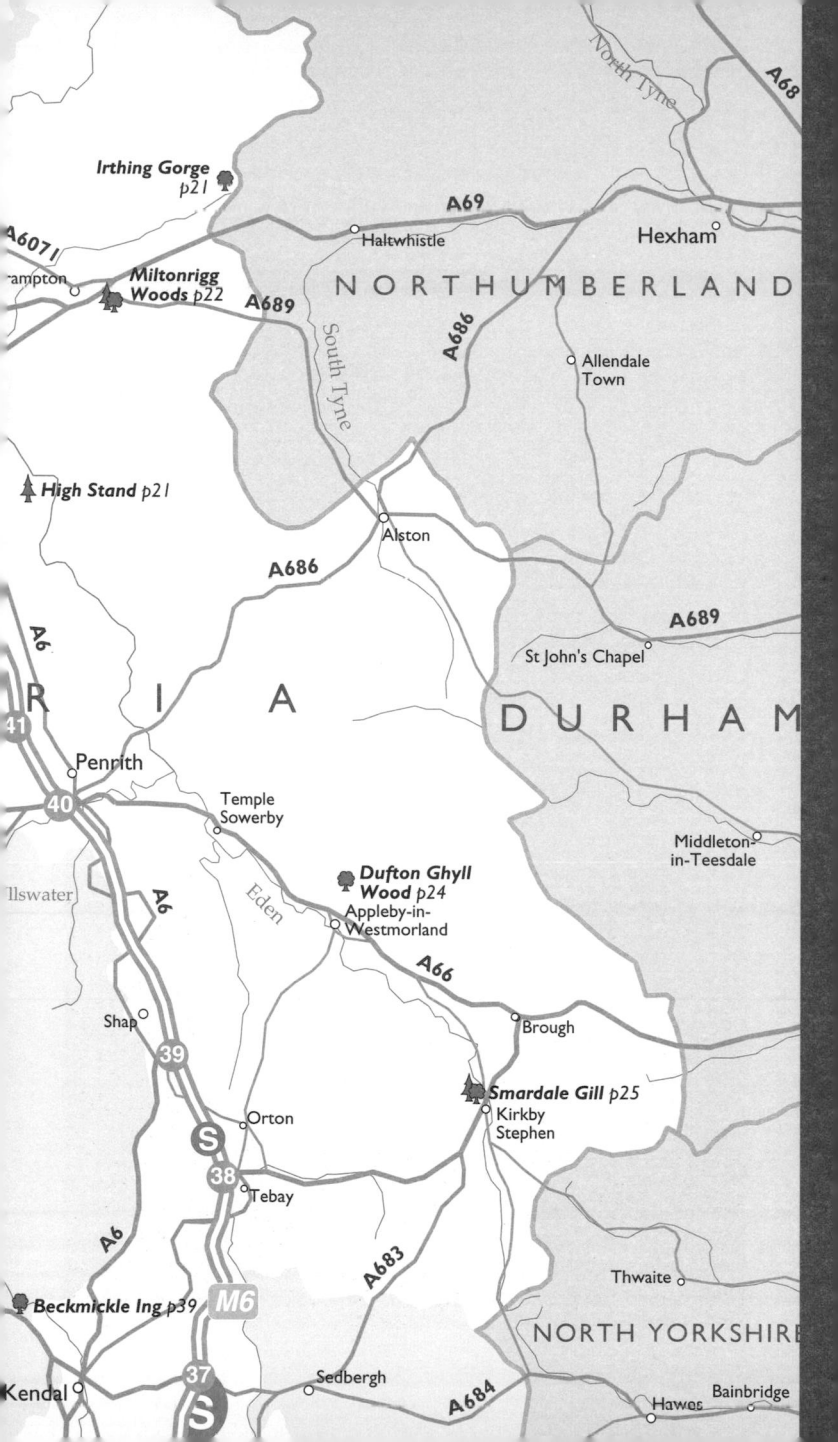

Irthing Gorge *p21*

A6071

~ampton

Miltonrigg Woods *p22*

A689

North Tyne

A68

A69

Haltwhistle

Hexham

N O R T H U M B E R L A N D

A686

Allendale Town

South Tyne

High Stand *p21*

A686

Alston

A689

St John's Chapel

D U R H A M

R   I   A

41

Penrith

Temple Sowerby

Middleton-in-Teesdale

Eden

Dufton Ghyll Wood *p24*

Appleby-in-Westmorland

A66

llswater

A6

40

Brough

Shap

39

Smardale Gill *p25*

Kirkby Stephen

Orton

S

38

Tebay

A683

Thwaite

A6

Beckmickle Ing *p39*

M6

N O R T H   Y O R K S H I R E

Kendal

37

S

Sedbergh

A684

Hawes

Bainbridge

Finglandrigg Wood National Nature Reserve

Carlisle

The site is well signed from the Haverlands Green lay-by on B5307 Carlisle to Kirkbride road. (NY282572)

97HA (240ACRES) SSSI

English Nature

Wonderful for walks, Finglandrigg National Nature Reserve is an island of rich habitats in an otherwise featureless landscape.

One of the largest areas of semi-natural woodland on the Solway Plain, the reserve is made up of a mosaic of habitats that support a range of wildlife, including numerous

Finglandrigg

bird species and red squirrels, that thrive among the Scots pine.

Formerly agricultural land and peat bog, the reserve is a mixture of naturally regenerated birch, rowan, willow, oak and beech, broken up with sections of pine which have developed from original planting in the early 19th century to become natural looking stands on the woodland edges.

Visitors can spend many hours exploring the woodland and adjoining lowland heath of Little Bampton Common via an excellent network of footpaths and enjoy one of many lovely picnic spots.

Most walks are on level ground, though off the surfaced tracks the going can get muddy. Exploration is helped by a good supply of information panels.

Irthing Gorge

Gilsland
Either park in the village of Gilsland and follow the public footpath which passes Wardrew House or turn off B6318 in Gilsland toward Gilsland Spa. If you can find a space to park near the hotel you can walk into the wood from here. (NY634685)
34HA (84 ACRES) SSSI NP
The Woodland Trust

History, romance, spectacular scenery, watersports and an abundance of wildlife – Irthing Gorge has it all.

This ancient woodland, a Site of Special Scientific Interest, forms part of a mosaic of wildlife habitats. It lines the steep sides of a deep gorge chiselled by the fast-flowing River Irthing. At its head is a waterfall known as Crammel Linn. Now the Woodland Trust is planting native trees on adjoining grassland to buffer and extend the ancient woodland.

Red squirrels and badgers inhabit the gorge, alongside a varied bird population and a rich mix of woodland plants. Yew grows on the cliff edges while ash dominates the lower slopes and birch is to be found on higher ground.

The gorge lies four miles north of Gilsland, one of 19th-century Britain's most fashionable spa resorts. Still popular, its scenery is as romantic as ever.

Kingmoor Nature Reserve

Carlisle
Go north on A7 over River Eden, turn left at second traffic lights into Etterby Road and follow road (becomes Kingmoor Road) to urban fringe. The reserve is opposite a large warehouse. (NY388578)
43HA (106ACRES)
Carlisle City Council

High Stand

Armathwaite/Wetheral
Follow signs for Armathwaite off A6. Take first left in village and continue for 2.5km (1.5 miles). At sign to FE car park turn right. Car park is 1.6km (1 mile) on the left. (NY498495)
250HA (618ACRES)
Forestry Commission

Miltonrigg Woods

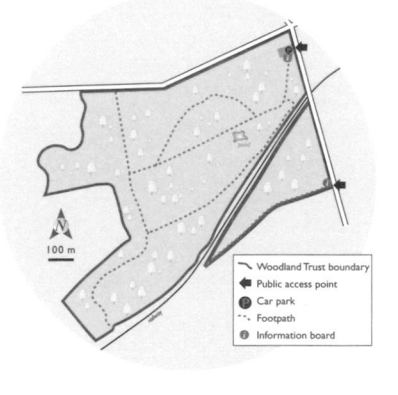

Brampton

A69 from Brampton, turn right on
minor road heading south, car park 30m
on right. (NY559612)
63HA (157ACRES)
The Woodland Trust

Just a few miles south of historic Hadrian's Wall is a landmark of Nature's making – Miltonrigg Wood, an outstanding feature of the Cumbrian landscape.

A network of paths lead you through this peaceful ancient woodland. The wood is accessible for all abilities and includes a surfaced route, which is suitable for wheelchair users and visitors with buggies.

The wood is dominated by wonderful beech and oak trees, many over 100 years old. Oak timber harvested from this site is reputed to have been used for the rebuilding of sections of York Minster roof. Some areas were planted with conifers in the post-war years and rhododendron dominated the wood in the past. The Woodland Trust is undertaking a careful programme of work to restore the woodland's ancient communities.

Elsewhere, areas have been left undisturbed allowing the dead and dying trees to create habitats for small insects and mammals. Visitors may be lucky enough to spot the occasional roe deer.

More than 200 species of flowering plant grow here – including seven species of sedge and five of rush as well as wood sorrel, wood anemone, bluebell and early purple orchid along the path edges. Marsh cinquefoil, which takes its name from the five sharp purple petals of its bloom can also be spotted by the keen eye in wetter sections of the wood.

Miltonrigg is alive with birds including kestrel, sparrowhawk, tawny owl, great spotted woodpecker, redstart and coal tit among the more common woodland birds. Summer visitors might be lucky enough to witness the evening display flight of a woodcock.

A pond at the heart of the wood provides a habitat for dragonflies, toads and newts.

Dufton Ghyll Wood

Dufton

On the steep sides of Dufton Gill, just
south of the village of Dufton, near
Appleby. (NY685251)
10HA (26ACRES) AONB SSSI
The Woodland Trust

Dufton Ghyll Wood is one of
the few remaining northwest
outposts for the native red
squirrel.

Lining the steep, sheltered
sides of a valley on the western
edge of the Pennines, the site is
as exciting for its geology as
much as the trees. It is
designated regionally
important for St Bee's
sandstone (a deposit laid down
by a river flowing through a
vast desert plain) – hailed as 'the

Dufton Ghyll

best exposure in the Eden Valley'.

By the time the Woodland
Trust took on the site in 1980
most of the trees had been
felled but a replanting
programme has seen the
surviving mature beech, oak,
sycamore, sweet chestnut and
elm complemented by young,
native broadleaves.

In spring the ground is covered
with the brightly coloured blooms
of winter aconite, daffodils,
wood anemones, bluebells,
pignut and angelica – with
mosses, ferns and liverworts in
damper areas.

Aira Force

Glenridding/Pooley Bridge
Well signposted from the A592 along
the west shore of Ullswater. (NY401200)
100HA (247ACRES) NP
The National Trust

Woodland tends to take a back seat to waterfalls at Aira Force (see p35). But the woods, lovely in their own right, are well worth exploring on a visit to this spectacular landscape.

The area, already a popular tourist spot in the late 18th century, became a celebrated destination during the 19th century when the Howard family created an arboretum on the hillside below.

The arboretum is dominated by conifers including some splendid Douglas fir and cedars and a spectacular giant Sitka spruce.

Take advantage of the well surfaced paths to climb up the hillside towards High Force. Mosses, lichens and ferns thrive in the moist air alongside the churning waters and often festoon oaks growing alongside hazel and birch trees.

There is plenty to explore beyond the falls and woods, not least the alder woods of Gowbarrow where you might spot red squirrels among the trees and dippers along the becks where primroses grow.

Smardale Gill

Kirkby Stephen

Turn off A685 (signposted Waitby and Smardale) approx 800m (0.5 mile) south of Kirkby Stephen. Follow signs to Smardale taking first turning left and then second turning left to car park.

(NY738083)
20HA (49ACRES) SSSI
Cumbria Wildlife Trust

Dramatic Smardale Gill is full of interest, where part of the old Stainmore railway line leads visitors through a peaceful landscape with only the river, birds and sheep supplying background noises.

Access is via a 'green tunnel' created by the trees and scrub that now enclose this stretch of the old railway line.

The walk follows the steep, densely wooded and flora-rich valley of Scandal Beck while, higher up, the Smardale viaduct adds drama and panoramic views are provided as trees give way to pasture.

The woodland is rich in wildlife – including red squirrel and roe deer – and a wonderful array of flora such as orchids and harebell. St John's wort grows alongside the railway cutting, attracting the rare Scotch Argus butterfly.

Within the reserve, the wood opens out, providing bird's eye views across the valley to the hills beyond. Permissive paths allow circular walks incorporating more open grassland areas.

Dodd Wood

Bassenthwaite/Keswick

Signposted from the A591 from
Keswick at Mirehouse. (NY245273)
260HA (643ACRES) SSSI NP
Forestry Commission

Gentle strolls, strenuous
walks, stunning lakeland and
mountain views – all can be
enjoyed with a visit to Dodd
Wood.

Planted with conifers in the
1920s, the mixed plantations
have been softened through
more recent, sensitive
management which is designed
to complement the Cumbrian
landscape.

A network of paths and rides
through the plantation provide
easy, sheltered walking by the
towering firs of Skill Beck and
Longside Wood. The paths are
well made and generally easy
underfoot, taking in broadleaf
glades and cool conifer
avenues.

The climb up to the top of
the fell is more strenuous but
from here you can enjoy wonderful views of Derwent Water
and the hills of Dumfries and
Galloway.

Plan a visit before the end of
summer and you may be
rewarded with the sight of an
osprey. If the weather is good,
the birds can be observed from
a special viewpoint across the
lake.

Whinlatter Forest Park

Braithwaite/Keswick

Follow signs from A66 Keswick to
Cockermouth Road. (NY210250)
1200HA (2966ACRES) NP
Forestry Commission

Whinlatter Forest Park is the
place to go if you're looking
for an all-weather woodland
experience – lots of interesting
walks, recreation activities and
stunning views from every
level.

This was the Forestry
Commission's first Lake
District planting in 1919,
later extended to create
Thornthwaite Forest.

Sitka spruce plantations
tower up to 1,700 feet above
you with larch, Douglas fir,
hemlock and red cedar on the
lower levels and broadleaves
bordering roads and rides.

Today, thinning and planting
work is improving the look of
the maturing forest, well used
for walks, cycling, orienteering
and timber production.

A series of well waymarked
routes provide opportunities to

Dodd Wood

escape the crowds and explore areas of broadleaves, conifer stands and open glades. Many lead to the summits of surrounding fells, others provide sheltered walking and the chance to observe wildlife.

During the breeding season you can enjoy live CCTV pictures of ospreys from the Whinlatter Visitor Centre.

Mirehouse and Catstocks Woods

Bassenthwaite/Keswick
Mirehouse is off the A59. Follow signs to Mirehouse from A66 at Keswick.
(NY236282)
13HA (32ACRES) SSSI
Mr J Fryer-Spedding

🅿️ ♿ 🖼️ 🔲 👫 ⛺ £ 🎯

Lanthwaite Wood

Lorton, south of Cockermouth
Take the B5289 from Cockermouth through Lorton towards Loweswater. Car park on left just past Scale Hill.
(NY150216)
28HA (69ACRES)
The National Trust

🅿️ ♿ 🖼️

Ennerdale Forest

Ennerdale Bridge
Follow road out of Ennerdale Bridge
toward lake for 6.5km (4 miles) to
Bowness Knot. (NY110153)
2674HA (6609ACRES) SSSI
Forestry Commission

Providing a striking backdrop
to stunning Cumbrian lakeland
scenery, Ennerdale Forest has
much to offer those willing to
leave the forest road and explore.

One of the region's largest
conifer forests, Ennerdale was
planted in the 1920s and is
dominated by larch, Scots pine

Miterdale Forest

and Sitka. But this huge site is
much more attractive than it
first seems – as a walk within
the woodland reveals.

Since the 1970s, work has
been carried out to mould a
forest more in tune with the
Cumbrian landscape and there
are areas of broadleaved woodland – by the lake, beside becks
and along forest rides – that
add variety to the scene.

These can be discovered by
following the waymarked trails
– strong boots recommended –
that provide wonderful views.
One of these – the Smithy
Beck Trail – is a delightful
short walk past the beck,
which can easily be extended
to take in broadleaf areas.

Miterdale Forest

Eskdale Green
From A595 take minor road to Eskdale.
Approx 800m (0.5 mile) past Bower
House Inn take minor road on left –
this leads past the school and into
Miterdale. (NY147012)
321HA (793ACRES)
Forestry Commission

Standing along the banks of the
River Mite is Miterdale Forest,
a conifer-dominated woodland
where the landscape changes
frequently.

Maturing trees lend
attraction to much of the site,
as a walk along the good
network of paths reveals. A
programme of felling and
replanting brings regular
changes to the area.

In the valley the woodland is
fairly open and pleasant to
walk through.

Tucked away on the side of
the valley are the oak woods of
Porterthwaite where coarse
Eskdale granite gives the
hillside a rocky feel and the
wood floor is clothed in mossy
boulders, ferns and carpets of
bilberry. On the edge of this
section a delightful packhorse
bridge crosses the river.

The woodland is dissected
by miniature fern-lined ravines,
cut by becks as they tumble
down towards the river. This is
a particularly lovely area of
woodland – equally good for a
quiet stroll or as part of a
longer expedition.

Blengdale Forest

Gosforth
Take Wasdale Road from Gosforth and
turn left by Walkmill Garden Centre
before road bends right to cross bridge.
Continue along this road until you
reach the parking area on the right.
(NY090070)
422HA (1043ACRES)
Forestry Commission

Giggle Alley

Eskdale Green
Follow signs to Eskdale Green from
A595. The wood is just past Eskdale
Green post office and stores.
(NY142001)
9HA (22ACRES)
Forestry Commission

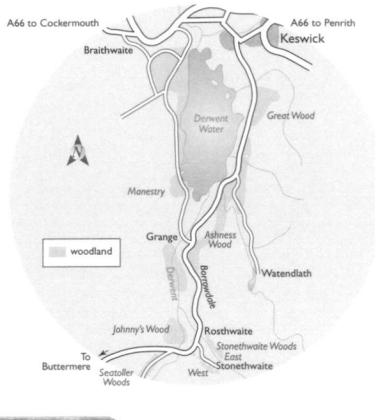

Borrowdale Woods

Keswick

From A527 take B5289 to Borrowdale. Ashness Wood is the largest area of wood in the middle section of the valley. There are three car parks that can be used to visit different parts of the wood. (NY254168)

650HA (1,607ACRES) SSSI NP

The National Trust

The wet Cumbrian climate has shaped a unique and spectacular woodland experience. Borrowdale Woods, nuzzling Derwent Water and stretching from Keswick to Seathwaite, are the region's own rainforests.

Extending over 650 hectares, this complex of upland oakwood contains lush lichen and moss-covered trees growing dramatically on steep, boulder-strewn slopes.

The woods were intensively managed for centuries to support local industry but later neglected. Sheep grazing prevented regrowth and this was followed by limited conifer planting. Work is ongoing to revitalise the woods by encouraging natural regeneration.

Each of the woods has its own character and atmosphere, thanks to different manage-ment methods employed in the past, with flora and fauna changing along with the gradient.

The area known as Lodore-Troutdale or Ashness Wood contains ancient woodland and is important for birds and insects, particularly the hairy wood ant. Red deer can often be seen. An array of short walks is possible, using a variety of paths and tracks, including a half-mile walk, suitable for wheelchairs and buggies, to the Bowderstone – a huge, impres-sive glacial boulder.

Great Wood, a mixture of conifers and ancient woodland, is renowned for the tree-dwelling lichens that thrive in its heart. Conditions vary from the lake shore where willow and alder dominate to drier fellside areas with oak and ash. Many routes lead through the wood including a path along to Walla Crag with its wonderful views of Borrowdale and Derwent Water.

Beautiful to walk through, Johnny's Wood is littered with moss-covered boulders overhung by branches of mature oak and provides good views across the valley. It is these sumptuous mosses, lichens, liverworts and ferns that give the wood its unique and rare character.

Manesty Wood, on the shores of Derwent Water, is a mixed broadleaf and conifer woodland whose well-surfaced paths allow good access to the shore for buggies and wheelchairs.

Stanley Ghyll

Stanley Ghyll

Eskdale Green
Follow signs to Eskdale Green from
A595. Just beyond village turn left
towards Boot. 400m (0.25 mile) past the
Beckfoot Halt Hotel take the small turn
right to Trough House Bridge (war
memorial on right). Car park on left
past bridge. (NY171003)
9HA (22ACRES) NP
Lake District National Park Authority

Short but dramatic, easy but
exciting, a walk through the
woodland of Stanley Ghyll is
an experience everyone – particularly children – can enjoy.

Part of the Dalegarth

amenity woods, the site is
made up of contrasting oak
and conifers. A stand of
conifers marks the start of a
short but scenic walk.

The path follows the beck up
the valley to a small, steep-
sided gorge where water
tumbles over Eskdale granite in
a series of falls and pools.

Though easy to tackle along
established paths, care is
needed towards the top of the
gorge where paths narrow and
the rocks can get slippery.

Visitors can incorporate
Stanley Ghyll as part of a
longer exploration of the
Dalegarth estate. A footpath
follows a lovely stretch of
the River Esk toward the
woodland higher up the valley.
A visit to the miniature railway
which runs from Dalegarth to
Ravenglass could add a further
dimension.

Muncaster Estate

Ravenglass
Signposted from A595 coast road.
(SD103965)
77HA (190ACRES)
Muncaster Estate

Family groups who remain
undaunted by the prospect of a
climb will find their exertions
well rewarded on a visit to the
Muncaster Estate.

The ornamental woodlands, set within the grounds of Muncaster Castle itself, provide miles of woodland walks with features to enthral everyone from the young child to the keen horticulturalist.

The amenity woods stretch across hills, enjoying a wonderful position overlooking the valley and providing views across to the fells beyond.

Many of the woodlands have fine tree specimens to discover – including some huge beeches and impressive conifers which add drama to the site.

Elsewhere in the castle grounds there is much to keep younger visitors amused, including owls and a Meadow Vole Maze.

Paths are rough, uneven and sometimes steep and can become boggy in wet weather – so boots are recommended for your visit.

Hardknott Forest

Broughton in Furness
Turn right off A595 from Broughton, just before River Duddon, signed Ulpha. Follow signs to Ulpha then Seathwaite – keep going towards Hardknott Pass – forest is on the left.
(SD234996)
629HA (1,555ACRES) SSSI
Forestry Commission

Hardknott Forest is full of variety – with open glades, rocky crags, rides, streams, bogs and dense woodland providing striking contrasts.

Choose your route from short circular walks along the valley bottom and lower slopes to longer, more strenuous climbs to the open Harter Fell. Take a breather here and enjoy some beautiful views across the Duddon Valley and north to the central Lakeland fells.

The plantations are mainly coniferous but there is an area of sessile oak woodland near to the River Duddon.

Behind the evolution of the site is a careful programme of planting by the Forestry Commission which began in the 1940s.

The resulting mixture is more varied and attractive than many older Lake District plantations and can be enjoyed as part of a wider tour of other woodlands in the valley such as Rainsbarrow, on next page.

Low Wood 🔲

Ulpha

On western slope of Duddon Valley, southwest of the Lake District National Park. (SD203943)

11HA (28ACRES) SSSI

The Woodland Trust

This ancient woodland is set on steep slopes of the Duddon Valley and is part of a large series of woodlands.

Oak, birch and sycamore grow on the lower slopes of the wood together with hazel, holly and rowan. Higher up, on land previously planted with conifers, a young woodland of oak, ash, alder, hazel, rowan and holly is emerging.

The woodland floor holds plenty of interest. At one moment an abundance of knee-high ferns and the next, bluebell, violet and wild daffodil add a mass of spring colour. Look too for wood ant colonies which occur frequently throughout.

The site was previously managed through coppicing to provide wood for the local bobbin mills as well as charcoal for a forge and blast furnace at Duddon Bridge.

As the woodland is steep and rocky and has no formal paths, visitors are urged to take special care when exploring.

Rainsbarrow 🔲

Broughton in Furness

Turn right off A595, near Broughton, just before River Duddon, signed Ulpha. Follow signs to Ulpha. Rainsbarrow entrance by post office in village. (SD190926)

50HA (124ACRES) SSSI

Forestry Commission

A typical Lake District woodland mix of oak, ash, birch, elm and hazel, it has the additional bonus of offering lovely views across the Duddon Valley.

Children will find particular delight watching the wood ants, a species characteristic to the valley which nest in large numbers along the footpath.

And if you take a circular walk through the wood up onto the open fell, you can enjoy a panorama of the Lake District fells, stretching south to Morecambe Bay.

A management programme by the Forestry Commission, which includes thinning and coppicing, is restoring the diversity of the woods and conserving the array of ground flora – among them bluebells, ramsons and primroses.

The woodland route follows narrow paths and wide rides which can get muddy so boots are recommended.

Aira Force (see p24)

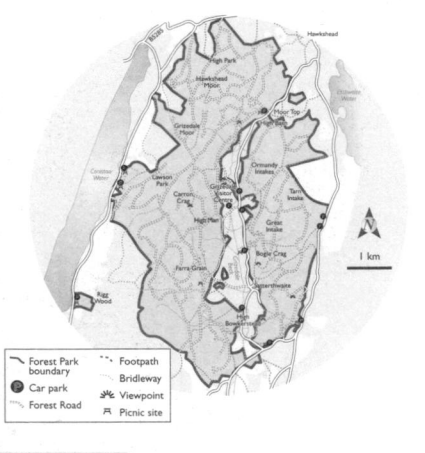

Grizedale Forest Park

Hawkshead

From the north: A591 to Ambleside, leave Ambleside A593 to Langdale/Coniston. First left B5286 to Hawkshead. By-pass Hawkshead follow B5286 south, first right, Tourist sign 'Theatre in the Forest', follow to Grizedale approx 3km (2 miles).

From the south: M6 junction 36 take A591. First exit A590, Barrow follow A590 past Newby Bridge Haverthwaite cross-roads, turn right, tourist signs 'Grizedale Forest Park', follow signs for Satterthwaite/Grizedale. (SD335945) 2447HA (6,048ACRES) NP

Forestry Commission

Situated between the lakes of Coniston and Windermere, Grizedale Forest Park provides a perfect introduction to anyone looking for their first woodland experience.

The name Grizedale means 'valley where young pigs are kept' and was first recorded in the early 14th century; however, the land was being used long before this date. In the 11th century the forest belonged to the monks of Furness Abbey who coppiced the oak wood to supply the abbey with a continuous supply of timber and firewood.

Extending to almost 12 square miles, this former timber plantation is set within a delightful Lakeland valley and is the largest forest within the Lake District. It is managed by the Forestry Commission for the benefit of wildlife and for visitors who can enjoy a range of recreational activities including cycle routes and orienteering courses.

While maturing conifers dominate, there are areas of indigenous hardwoods including sessile oak, birch and rowan. Wildlife includes red and roe deer and a variety of birds such as woodcock, nightjars, pied flycatchers, green woodpeckers and buzzards.

Delightful sculptures, sited throughout, were created by artists working in residence at Grizedale and made the forest internationally famous. It would take several days to see all the works of art. However, a series of well-marked routes of varying degrees of difficulty – from the all-ability Ridding Wood trail, to the demanding Silurian Way – allow visitors to discover these at a pace that suits them best.

Visitors flock to enjoy the miles of footpaths and forest rides, but the forest is successful in absorbing them unobtrusively.

There is a visitor centre with gallery, artist workshops, cafe, adventure playground, cycle hire facility and information point. A presentation in the visitor centre depicts the story of the forest from wildwood to the various roles it plays today.

There is also a theatre in the forest that presents a wide range of events including dance, classical, jazz, drama, variety and folk concerts.

In 2003 'Go Ape' arrived at Grizedale. This high rope course provides a challenging aerial adventure.

Grizedale provides a wonderful example of how well-managed, mature plantation woods can provide a variety of enjoyable experiences for large numbers of visitors of all ages.

Claife Woods

Beckmickle Ing

Hawkshead

Either approach on the B5285 Hawkshead to Windermere Ferry road, National Trust car park at foot of Ferry Hill or via road from High Wray village to the lake, car park at Red Nab. (SD385995) 230HA (568ACRES) NP

The National Trust

Set atop a hillside overlooking stunning Lake Windermere, Claife Woods is a large mixed woodland next to the Forestry Commission plantations on Claife Heights, with its panoramic views.

The walking is good and the woodland attractive and varied, ranging from dense woods on the lower slopes where you will encounter oak, birch, alder, holly and yew with some stands of larch.

Higher up they give way to a patchwork of woodlands and more open areas where Scots pine grow on the thin soil of the rocky knolls. Here, the landscape is dotted with small mires and tarns.

An extensive network of footpaths runs through the woods, allowing visitors to choose between an easy route along the shore of the lake to more strenuous walks up through the woods. Near the top are more open areas which lead to a viewpoint at the summit of Claife Heights.

Beckmickle Ing

Burneside
On the bank of the River Kent, just east of the village of Staveley, near Kendal. (SD490979)
4HA (9ACRES) SSSI
The Woodland Trust

Birdsong, bluebells and beauty – Beckmickle Ing, on the banks of the River Kent, has it all.

This is a well-loved ancient woodland site on the border of the Lake District National Park, as popular with visitors as with locals. A visit here can be combined with one of many walk routes in the area, including the Dalesway long distance path.

Inside the wood, where roe deer roam and red squirrel may be spotted, is a rich mix of broadleaves and a wonderfully diverse range of ground flora. Take in the sights and smells of ramson, lords and ladies, moschatel, pignut and Solomon's seal.

On the banks of the river, where nationally important crayfish and mussel populations live, are rushes, hemlock, water-dropwort and the yellow globeflower.

If you are lucky you might spot resident great spotted woodpeckers or spy dippers and common sandpiper around the riverbank.

Rayrigg Wood

Windermere
The wood is east of the A592, north of Windermere. (SD404975)
14HA (35ACRES)
Pattinsons (Windermere) Ltd

Skelghyll Wood

Ambleside
800m (0.5 mile) south of Ambleside on A591, turn left up to Stagshaw Gardens. (NY380028)
38HA (94ACRES)
The National Trust

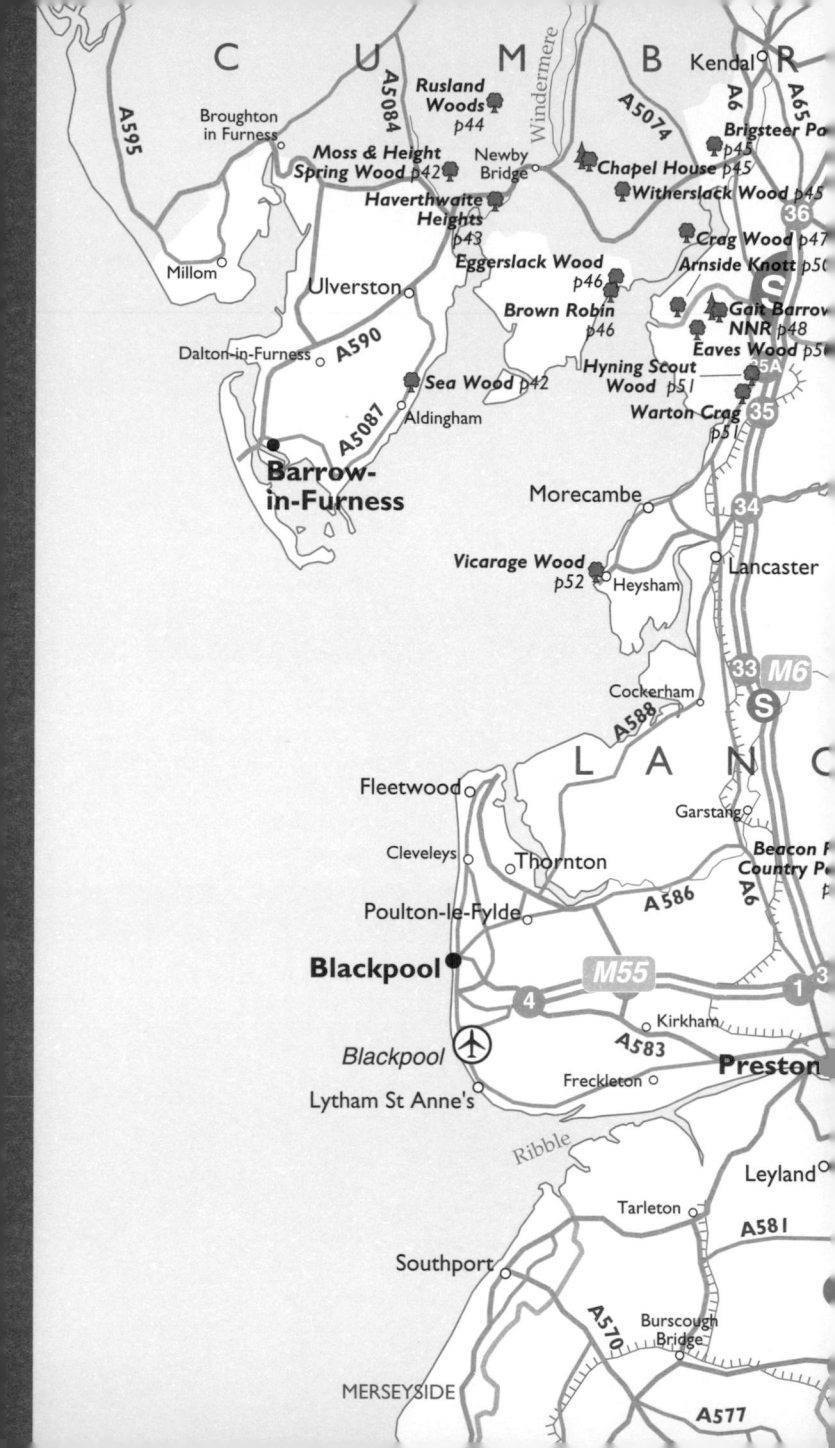

C U M B R

A595

A5084

Broughton
in Furness

**Rusland
Woods**
p44

Kendal

A6

A65

Brigsteer Pa
p45

A5074

Moss & Height
Spring Wood p42

Newby
Bridge

Chapel House *p45*

Witherslack Wood *p45*

**Haverthwaite
Heights**
p43

36

Millom

Eggerslack Wood
p46

Crag Wood *p47*

Arnside Knott *p5C*

Ulverston

Brown Robin
p46

**Gait Barrov
NNR** *p48*

Dalton-in-Furness

A590

A5087

Sea Wood *p42*

Aldingham

**Hyning Scout
Wood** *p51*

Eaves Wood *p5(*

5A

Warton Crag
p51

35

**Barrow-
in-Furness**

Morecambe

34

Vicarage Wood
p52

Heysham

Lancaster

33 **M6**

S

Cockerham

A588

L A N C

Fleetwood

Garstang

Cleveleys

Thornton

**Beacon F
Country Pε**
p

A586

A6

Poulton-le-Fylde

Blackpool

M55

4

Kirkham

Blackpool

A583

Preston

Lytham St Anne's

Freckleton

Ribble

Leyland

Tarleton

A581

Southport

Burscough
Bridge

A570

MERSEYSIDE

A577

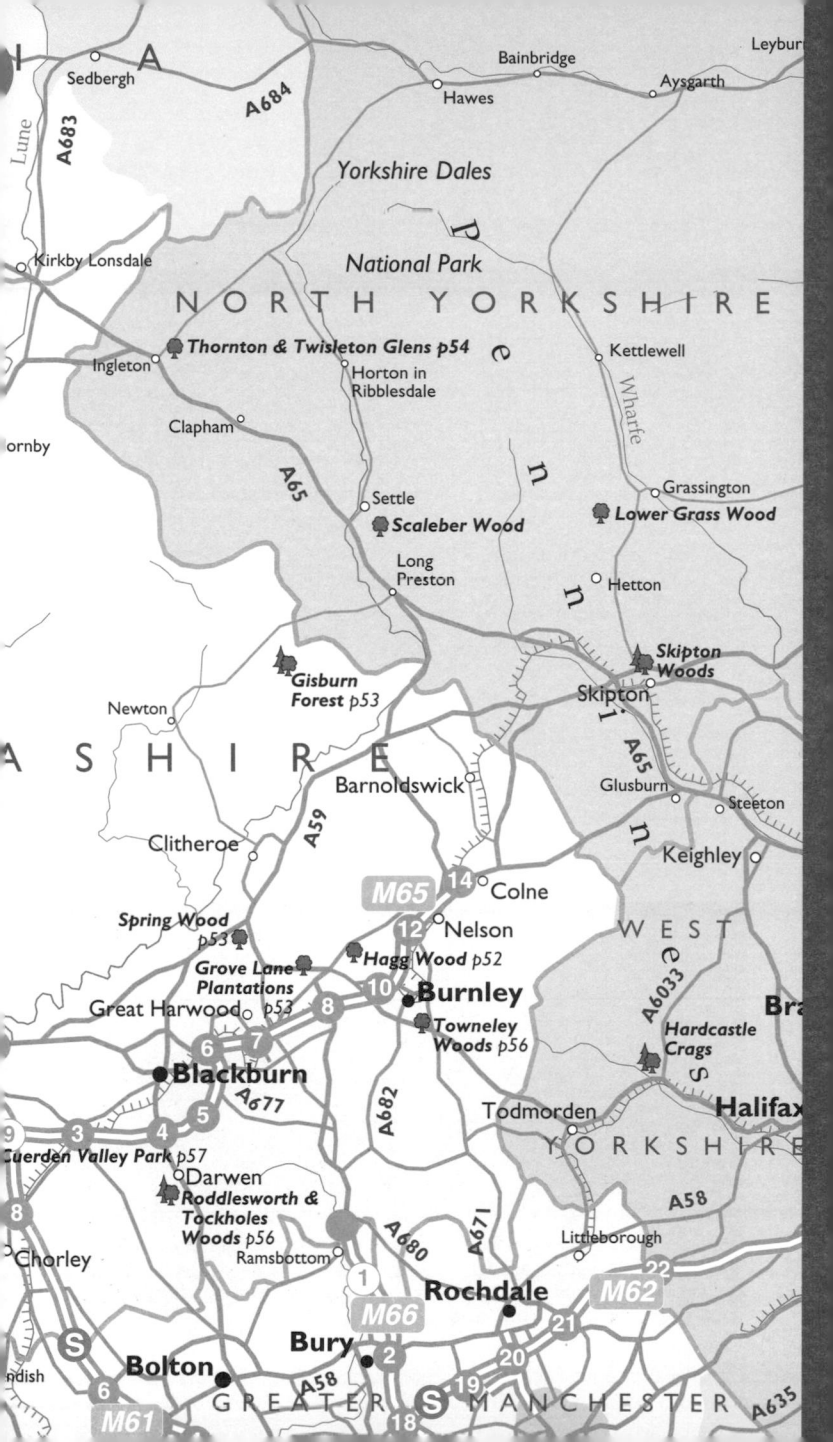

Moss & Height Spring Wood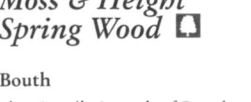

Bouth

3km (2 miles) north of Bouth and A590, car park on left. (SD324863)

19HA (48ACRES)

The Woodland Trust

History is never far away in Moss and Height Spring Wood, near Ulverston in Cumbria.

The wood is believed to be at least 350 years old and the wide track that dissects it considered an old coffin route used by the people of Bouth to reach the church at Colton.

Most of the oak-dominated wood today is mixed coppice including hazel, birch and alder, with oak standards and mature yew trees. Several small

Moss and Height Spring Wood

streams meander through, creating mossy and boggy areas, while more than 2,000 metres of footpath criss-cross this well loved rural spot. The red squirrel is resident here.

A rich ground flora includes dog's mercury, bilberry, primrose, honeysuckle, violets and wild strawberry.

A conifer block in the west of Moss Wood has been replanted with native broadleaves and birch allowed to re-seed naturally. This recreation of native woodland is helping to restore the biodiversity of this ancient site.

Sea Wood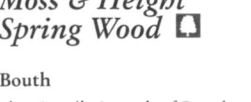

Bardsea

On northwest shore of Morecambe Bay, approximately 5km (3 miles) south of Ulverston at Bardsea. (SD293734)

23HA (58ACRES) SSSI

The Woodland Trust

⚆ 🏠 ℗ 🏛

A trip to the seaside can take on new meaning with a visit to Sea Wood. The woodland stands out against the northwest shore of Morecambe Bay and is edged by the shingle beach of Ulverston Sands.

The sea played an important part in the management of the wood – large oak timbers used to be floated at high tide to ship builders in Ulverston.

Today this ancient woodland is something of a county rarity and is recognised as the largest of its kind in South Cumbria.

Notable for its many old oak trees, the site is a rich broadleaf mix while the ground vegetation, denser in the northern wood, supports a host of small mammals. There is also a thriving population of small birds, blackbirds and thrushes. Look for the many types of lichen that add texture and colour to the tree trunks.

Haverthwaite Heights ⬛

Grange-over-Sands/Ulverston
Turn northwards off A590 at Haverthwaite crossroads, signposted to Bouth/Rusland/Grizedale, and then immediately right along old road. (SD342845)

78HA (193ACRES)
Lake District National Park
Authority

Haverthwaite Heights is a rich and interesting mix of ancient woodland set atop craggy, undulating hillside in the Lakeland fells around Windermere.

The higher sections of the woodland, topped with lovely gnarled mature Scots pine, are particularly attractive.

A short but delightful walk along a hillside path takes visitors up through the wood. Although steep in places, the going is not too difficult with plenty of chances to enjoy panoramic views over Morecambe Bay.

En route you encounter areas of mature larch and former conifer plantations now largely replanted with native broadleaves. Much of the site has broadleaf cover, with old oak coppice, birch and yew. Bracken, foxgloves and bluebells can be found on the woodland floor and as you climb higher you find bilberry too.

If you want to explore further, a permissive path through the wood to Backbarrow provides a circular walk and you can even take a trip along the valley on the Haverthwaite railway.

Rusland Woods

Rusland Woods

Newby Bridge

From A590 take turning signposted
Grizedale/Rusland. Follow signs for
approx 3km (2 miles). Rusland Woods
on right – lookout for LDNP sign.
(SD335893)
60HA (148ACRES)
Lake District National Park Authority

Wonderfully atmospheric,
Rusland Woods is a lovely site
to explore.

A rich mix of mainly open
broadleaved trees, with hand-
some, mature examples dotted
throughout, it looks as good in
the mist and rain as it does on
bright days with sun filtering
through the canopy.

Beech, yew and oak dominate
the woodland and one
wonderful old sweet chestnut
stands near the entrance gate.
Further up the hill a beautiful
mature spreading oak adds
drama to an already feature-
packed walk.

The path, while not surfaced,
makes for easy walking and is
well marked with white-
topped posts.

The famous Rusland beeches
line the road along the edge of
the woods. Many of the
ancient trees remain, although
some have been felled and
replanted to secure the future
of this attractive feature.

Within the woodland, rocky
outcrops run in parallel ridges up
the hillside, forming small cliffs.
Yew and occasionally beech trees
cling to rocks, their roots
snaking across the rock surface.

Brigsteer Park

Levens Village
Follow signs from A590 to Levens.
Pass through village and follow signs to
Brigsteer. Wood is 2.5km (1.5 miles)
after Levens. (SD488876)
34HA (83ACRES)
The National Trust

Mrs Humphry Ward brought
Brigsteer Park to the attention
of Victorians through her
novel 'Hellbeck of Bannisdale',
describing its magnificent daffodil display as being 'flung on
the fellside through a score of
acres'. You don't have to
restrict visits to the spring as
Brigsteer is a joy any time of
year.

Set on a limestone hillside
overlooking the Lyth valley,
this site provides a rich habitat
for birds, plants and insects –
including butterflies – with
plenty to offer the woodland
walker, whatever the season.

Splendid old yews intermix
with oak, ash, hazel and holly
with underplanted beech and
conifers now being thinned by
the National Trust in a bid to
restore a more natural balance.
Overgrown hazel is being
re-coppiced and felled timber
is left to rot to provide new
habitats for insects.

A network of wide tracks
and narrow winding paths provide ample opportunities to
explore, with wonderful views
over the Lyth valley and its
renowned damson orchards.

Witherslack Wood

Witherslack/Lindale
Turn off A590, following signs to
Witherslack. Continue north on minor
road for approx 1.6km (1 mile) to
Witherslack Hall. (SD433862)
400HA (989ACRES) SSSI
The Stanley Family

Chapel House

Newby Bridge
Head north on A592 towards
Windermere from A590 at Newby
Bridge. After 1.6km (1 mile) turn right
and head up hill for a further 1km.
Parking is on the right. The car park is
signed Gummer's How. Turn off A590
at sign to Staveley. Park on lay-by along
minor road from where there is access
to the plantation via a forest ride.
(SD397875)
333HA (823ACRES)
Forestry Commission

Eggerslack Wood

Grange over Sands
Turn off A590 south onto B5271
towards Grange. Wood is approx
1.6km (1 mile) on right. (SD408784)
47HA (116ACRES)
Forestry Commission

Ever changing and packed with
interest, Eggerslack Wood is
rich in plant, bird and insect
life. The visitor will find plenty
to observe and enjoy.

Good paths lead you
through predominantly mixed
broadleaved woodland where
you wander between birch,
ash, oak, holly, rowan, yew and
areas of hazel coppice. There
are also planted areas of beech,
larch and sycamore.

At the bottom of the wood is
a peaceful, shady hazel coppice.
Along the path the wood opens
out and sun slips through the
canopy of oak, birch, ash and
sycamore revealing dog's
mercury and ferns.

Up the hill, limestone
outcrops support common dog
violet, bluebell and woodrush
and, at the top, open grassland
makes a wonderful picnic spot
with panoramic views across
Morecambe Bay.

Gently descend through
woods of wild cherry and ash
and oak. The path passes a
lovely mature oak and a
wonderfully clear spring on
the way down.

Brown Robin

Grange over Sands
From mini roundabout near Grange
over Sands railway station take B5271,
access to reserve is 1km (0.75 mile) on
right. (SD411783)
13HA (32ACRES)
Cumbria Wildlife Trust

Evenly split between grassland
and woodland, Brown Robin
reserve is rich in wildlife and a
pleasure to explore.

The woods are at their most
spectacular in spring when
bluebells, ramsons, wild
daffodils and primroses carpet
the floor. Hart's tongue fern
and dog's mercury are also
seen growing here.

Interest is amplified by the
mosaic of habitats that make
up this site – from sunny open
grassland to deep, shady wood.
Stop off at one of a number of
great picnic spots and take time
to observe the array of wildlife
including roe deer, woodpeckers
and buzzards.

The underlying limestone
bedrock has produced a
distinctive mix of dominant
ash, hazel and yew with oak,
beech, sycamore and elm.

Walking is fairly easy and
the paths, which range from

farm tracks to narrow winding woodland routes lead to the top of the reserve from where panoramic views across Morecambe Bay can be enjoyed.

Crag Wood

Meathop
On the edge of Morecambe Bay Estuary in the Lake District National Park.
(SD457806)
4HA (9ACRES)
The Woodland Trust

Crag Wood is located on the edge of the Morecambe Bay estuary.

Precipitous limestone cliffs drop dramatically down to the estuary mudflats below. In the middle of the woodland a seasonal pond with yellow iris, bulrush and soft rush and edged with alder and willow attracts birdlife including mallard, heron, sparrowhawk, chiff-chaff, willow warbler and goldcrest.

Oak, birch, ash and cherry are all to be found in this ancient woodland. Keep your eye out too for the occasional mature yew tree. Beneath this canopy is a mix of hazel, hawthorn, blackthorn, holly and crab apple.

The woodland floor comes alive each spring with a fine display of bluebells and wood anemones. Yorkshire fog, wood sorrel, bugle and yellow pimpernel add their colour amongst trailing honeysuckle and bramble.

Access can be gained from the Cumbria Coastal Way to the north of the wood. The woodland boasts a circular route with a wonderful view point across the bay to the village of Arnside.

Crag Wood

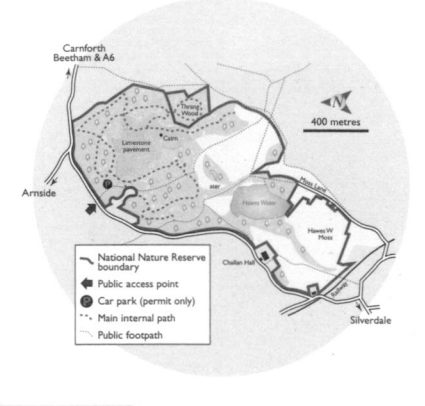

Gait Barrows NNR

Silverdale

From A6 follow signs to Leighton Moss RSPB reserve. After passing reserve turn right at T-junction past Silverdale station and continue, ignoring minor road to left and road to right, over railway line, turning left to Waterslack after approx 1km (0.75 mile). Entrance to Gait Barrows 1.6km (1 mile) on right. (SD478773)

117HA (289ACRES) AONB SSSI

English Nature

Casual visitors and naturalists alike will find plenty of interest at Gait Barrows National Nature Reserve – not least the views across the Arnside and Silverdale Area of Outstanding Natural Beauty.

This delightfully sheltered site boasts perhaps the country's finest example of limestone pavement supporting a miniature woodland of stunted yew, ash, elm, rowan and hazel trees. These grow very slowly in the limestone cracks – known as 'grikes' – where root growth is restricted and water in short-supply – some of the trees may well be over 300 years old.

Two waymarked trails take the visitor gently through woodland, surrounding meadows, fen, reedbeds and to the lakes of Little Hawes Water and Hawes Water. This is easy walking but care should be taken on the limestone, particularly in wet conditions.

Rare butterflies, such as the high brown fritillary, pearl bordered fritillary and Duke of Burgundy, might be seen here. It is worth spending some time peering into the limestone grikes to discover the range of plantlife sheltering here. Among the many rarities are ferns and the dark red helleborine.

Surrounding the open pavement are mixed woodland areas of oak and ash with a dense understorey of spindle, guelder rose, dogwood and hazel. Thrang Wood is a haunting area of ancient yew woodland littered with moss-covered boulders. Dark and cool, the wood is in startling contrast to the bright open pavement which slopes south and seems to radiate heat even on fairly overcast days.

An amazing 1,600 types of fungi and 800 moth species have been recorded in these woods. Wood ants are common particularly in the north of the reserve. Birdlife includes such notable species as the bittern and marsh harrier.

While the best time to visit for flowering plants is during spring and summer months, year-round interest is provided by the reserve's variety of woodland birds.

Arnside Knott

Arnside, Carnforth

From A6 at Milnthorpe take B5282 and
follow signs to Arnside and the Arnside
Knott. (SD456775)

107HA (264ACRES) AONB SSSI

The National Trust

There is a rich and varied
landscape to explore on
Arnside Knott, a 150 m (500 ft)
limestone hill with stunning
views across Morecambe Bay.

Noted for its rich flora and
butterflies, you can explore
several areas – each with its
own distinctive character.
Walking is easy through the
mosaic of woodland, scrub and
tussocky herb-rich grassland.

The summit is dotted with
the weathered stumps of larch
trees cut down in 1914.

Redhills Wood, clothing the
northern slopes, has a maze of
narrow paths and rides leading
you through a dense mix of oak,
hazel, holly and yew trees with
violets and primroses in spring.

Further round the hill, the
branches of splendid old yews
cast deep shadows while on the
lower slopes more open, mixed
oak woodland contrasts with
Redhills.

Circular walks can be
extended to take in nearby sites
of interest such as neighbouring
Heathwaite.

Eaves Wood

Silverdale

From A6 follow signs to Leighton Moss
RSPB reserve. Continue past reserve
take right at T-junction. Drive past Silverdale
station and continue to Eaves Wood car
park, 1 km (0.75 mile). (SD465758)

43HA (106ACRES) AONB SSSI

The National Trust

Children can enjoy discovering
circles of trees known as the
Ring o' Beeches, a stone tower
called the Pepperpot overlooking
Morecambe Bay – built for
Queen Victoria's golden jubilee
– and the ruins of a former
woodcutter's home.

A network of paths through
the site meander across open
areas of limestone then plunge
into dense ancient woodland.
Flowering plants, lichens and
insects associated with ancient
woodland thrive here. Moss
and fern covered limestone
outcrops emerge in parallel
ridges across the woodland floor.

Tall Scots pine reach high
into the canopy while beech
spread wide over a clear
woodland floor, turning it
golden each autumn.

Higher up, limestone areas
are home to a host of rare species
including the dark red helleborine
and bloody cranesbill and rare
butterflies such as the pearl
bordered fritillary.

Hyning Scout Wood

Hyning Scout Wood

Yealand Conyers

Lies between Yealand Conyers and
Warton, approx 8km (5 miles) west of
junction 35 of M6. (SD501735)
21HA (52ACRES) AONB
The Woodland Trust

A place of beauty and
atmosphere, you can stroll
beneath wonderful big beech
and sweet chestnuts dating
back maybe 200 years with
delightful spring carpets of
bluebells at your feet.

Much is ancient woodland –
a mixture of mature ash,
sycamore, sweet chestnut and
oak that has evolved on the clints
(limestone blocks) and grikes
(water-eroded gaps) of the
Arnside and Silverdale Area of
Outstanding Natural Beauty.

Rare ferns and flowers found
here include the downy
currant and the rigid buckler
fern. Red squirrels can still be
seen around Hyning and
browsing roe deer are often
spotted in the wood.

The remains of a limestone
kiln can be seen in the south of
the wood. Today the limestone
is legally protected from exca-
vation and damage.

Many well-used footpaths
provide good circular walks
and link up with routes across
neighbouring countryside,
including Warton Crag. Care
should be taken on the
limestone pavements which
can become slippery when wet.

Warton Crag

Carnforth

From junction 35A on M6 take A6
north. First left to Warton village and
left at crossroads in main street. Right
into Crag Road, at George Washington
pub, main car park 500m on right.
(SD493728)
35HA (87ACRES) AONB SSSI
Lancashire Wildlife Trust

Vicarage Wood

Morecambe
Leave M6 at junction 34, follow signs
for Heysham then brown tourist signs
for St Patricks Chapel. Park in pay and
display car park in Heysham.
(SD410617)
2HA (5ACRES)
The National Trust

Vicarage Wood was planted in
the 19th century in an idyllic
coastal headland setting.

Despite its small size, the
woodland is packed with
charm, character and history.
It is a great place for children
to explore, too.

The sycamore-dominated
wood offers shelter from the
sea breezes that sweep across
Morecambe Bay and makes a
wonderful contrast with the
neighbouring open headland.
Many trees on the seaward side
have been stunted by the wind.

Exposed low cliffs and
massive sandstone boulders
add drama and atmosphere.

There is evidence of human
activity dating back thousands
of years. Indeed, the headland
is one of Lancashire's most
important archaeological sites
and the wood itself houses a
rock-cut grave, probably linked
to an early Christian site near
the old chapel ruins on the cliffs.

Hagg Wood

Ightenhill
Junction 10 on M65, turn down
Ightenhill Park Lane and park 100m
before lane ends, in layby. Cross
Woodland Trust marked stile, just
before lane continues through gate as
bridleway. (SD817346)
5HA (14ACRES)
The Woodland Trust

Ancient woodland sites such
as Hagg Wood are rare in
Lancashire.

Set in an open landscape of
sheep grazed grassland, moors
and hills, this provides an
important wildlife haven. The
wood also extends down a
steep bank to the River Calder.

Packed into this small wood
are many distinct areas. In the
heart of the wood young birch,
oak, rowan, holly and sycamore
are regenerating surrounded by
a fringe of older mature
broadleaves.

Of the colourful variety of
flowering plants to be found
here, bluebell, wood anemone,
honeysuckle and enchanter's
nightshade indicate this is
indeed ancient woodland.
Meadowsweet, giant horsetail,
cuckoo pint and a variety of
ferns add to the wood's
undoubted appeal. Jay,
sparrowhawk, little owl and
kingfisher have been spotted.

Gisburn Forest

Settle/Clitheroe
Take A65 east towards Leeds, at Long
Preston take B6478 south to Slaidburn.
After 11km (7 miles) take right turn to
Gisburn (between Tosside and
Slaidburn). From west on A65 take
turning signposted Clapham Station,
Keasden near village of Clapham. Follow
minor road across Clapham Moor to
Forest. (SD745551-SD733565)
1236HA (3,055ACRES) AONB
Forestry Commission

Although Gisburn Forest is
in a fairly remote location,
surrounded by open countryside,
it is well worth the effort to get
there – particularly if you are a
keen naturalist or birdwatcher.

The expansive, mainly coniferous forest on the edge of the
Stocks Reservoir is one of the best
wildfowl sites in the northwest –
red-breasted merganser breed here.

Easy strolls can be enjoyed
along one of several waymarked
trails, cycleways and bridleways –
with lots of potential picnic spots.

Much of the plantation is
being harvested and the variety of
young and mature trees provide
various habitats. Visitors may
find interest in the replanted and
regenerating broadleaf areas.

Park Wood, an area of semi-
natural woodland along
Bottoms Beck, is particularly
good for plants and insects.

Gisburn

Water tumbles along the beck
while inside the woodland you
might spot titmice, finches and
even crossbills. The open rides
support a lovely variety of
flora including early purple
and spotted orchid.

Grove Lane Plantations

Padiham
Follow cycleway signs from A671
roundabout via Lune St, Holmes St,
Ingham St & Grove Lane. (SD800343)
7HA (17ACRES)
Burnley Borough Council

Spring Wood

Whalley
Immediately adjacent to A671 Whalley
by-pass. Signposted Spring Wood Picnic
Site. (SD741361)
16HA (40ACRES)
Lancashire County Council

Thornton & Twisleton Glens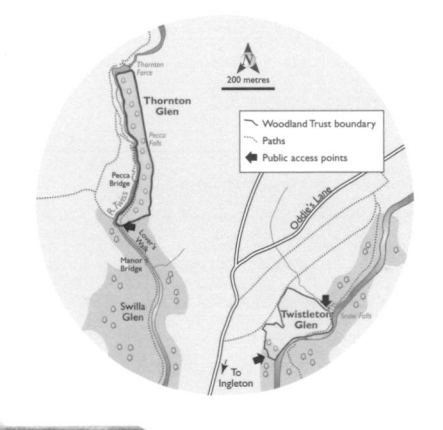

Ingleton

On the edge of Ingleton village parking is provided for the Waterfalls Walk (signposted) by the Ingleton Scenery Company, which charges for parking and access.

(SD695750/SD700742)

8 HA (20 ACRES) SSSI

The Woodland Trust

Ancient woodland is something of a rarity in North Yorkshire making Thornton and Twisleton Glens all the more valuable.

Situated on the banks of the River Twiss and River Doe, the two woods are part of a larger unbroken chain of ancient woodland following each river's course in the Yorkshire Dales National Park.

Ingleton had been known for its caves and mountain scenery since the second half of the 18th century, but the now famous waterfalls of the Ingleton Glens were hidden in tree-filled craggy ravines. So difficult were they to get to that even the farmers and quarrymen who earned their living nearby were unaware of their existence.

Both woods are accessed via the stunningly beautiful 7 km (4.5 miles) Waterfalls Walk from Ingleton. Since the late 19th century, visitors have enjoyed this route which includes ancient oak woodland, geological features and magnificent Dales scenery.

The walk leads you through spectacular landscapes of dramatic outcrops with cascades and waterfalls – the most famous being Thornton Force. There is a viewing area here where you can enjoy a picnic and watch the river fall 14 metres over limestone rocks in an impressive cascade. Also, don't miss Snow Falls beside Twisleton Glen. Look for lichens and soft mosses that thrive in the deep dark gullies.

The rock steps into which these glens have cut were formed because of the different resistance to erosion of the rocks lying each side of the great earth fractures known as the Craven Faults.

While visitors today will enjoy the rich mosaic of plants that cover Twisleton's woodland floor, a profusion of wild ferns, lilies of the valley and wild orchids once grew here. Unfortunately these were dug up during the 19th and 20th centuries and sold as souvenirs to visitors.

Towneley Woods

Towneley Woods

Burnley
Follow signs from M65 and A671 for
Towneley Hall Park. (SD855307)
20HA (49ACRES)
Burnley Borough Council

Woodland has existed in the
grounds of historic Towneley
Hall since 1400 but the visitor's
route is along paths laid out in
the 1800s when the grounds
were landscaped in classic
English style.

The legacy of this historical
background can be enjoyed
among the mixed native
broadleaves and exotic species
that populate the site today.
Look for sculptures created
along the walks here and at
nearby Grove Lane
Plantations, Padiham and in
the woods of Gawthorpe Hall.

Towering beech trees are a
feature of this woodland. The
many other surprises waiting

to be discovered include relics
from the 19th century such as
an arched passageway in
Thanet Lee Wood, a ha-ha,
rustic tunnels and the Monks
Well grotto.

The woodland itself is a mixture of exotic and native trees.
Soil changes throughout the
site are reflected in the variety
of ground flora – clay-loving
ramson in some sections contrasting with an abundance of
bluebells in more acidic areas.

*Roddlesworth &
Tockholes Woods*

Darwen
Take junction 3 off M65 and follow
A675 towards Bolton. Approx 4km (2.5
miles) after Abbey Village turn sharp
left down road signposted to Tockholes.
Park at visitor centre near the Royal
Arms. (SD665215)
195HA (482ACRES)
United Utilities

One of Lancashire's largest broadleaved woods, Roddlesworth includes such features as reservoirs, dark beech woods and attractive open moorland ideal for picnics.

Planted from 1904 by Liverpool Corporation to halt erosion of the valley sides, the site is dominated by a mix of oak, ash, beech, alder and pine. Today it is full of surprises, changing suddenly from dense plantations of gnarled beech trees to open areas of oak and birch.

Don't be put off by rather uninspiring names: Tockholes Number Two plantation is more engaging than its title suggests. Bluebells adorn the woodland floor and scent the air in spring and in the autumn fungi are prolific.

Several waymarked routes run through habitats that support spotted woodpecker, goldcrest, tree creeeper and wood warbler while the stream, flowing beneath small cliffs, draws kingfishers.

Cuerden Valley Park

Bamber Bridge

South of Preston, easy access from junctions 28 and 29 on M6. Follow brown tourist signs. (SD565238) 260HA (643ACRES)

Cuerden Valley Park Trust

Beacon Fell Country Park

Chipping

Signposted from A6 north of Preston. (SD565427)

87HA (215ACRES) AONB

Lancashire County Council

Set atop an isolated hill 873ft above sea level, this country park is popular with visitors who turn up in large numbers.

Despite this, it is easy to find a quiet walk or picnic spot on open moorland or in woodland clearings.

A variety of trees frame wonderful panoramic views from the Fell. Conifers used to dominate but these have been well thinned and replanted, allowing rowan, birch, alder and oak to emerge and create habitats for a rich variety of wildlife.

What makes this a delight to explore is the contrast between enclosed cool and shady plantations – with their subtle interplay of light and shadow – and the sunny stretches of open moorland. Wonderful in sunshine, it has interest even when the fell is shrouded in mist.

The site has something for everyone from gentle walking along a network of paths to mountain biking, orienteering and a sculpture trail to amuse children.

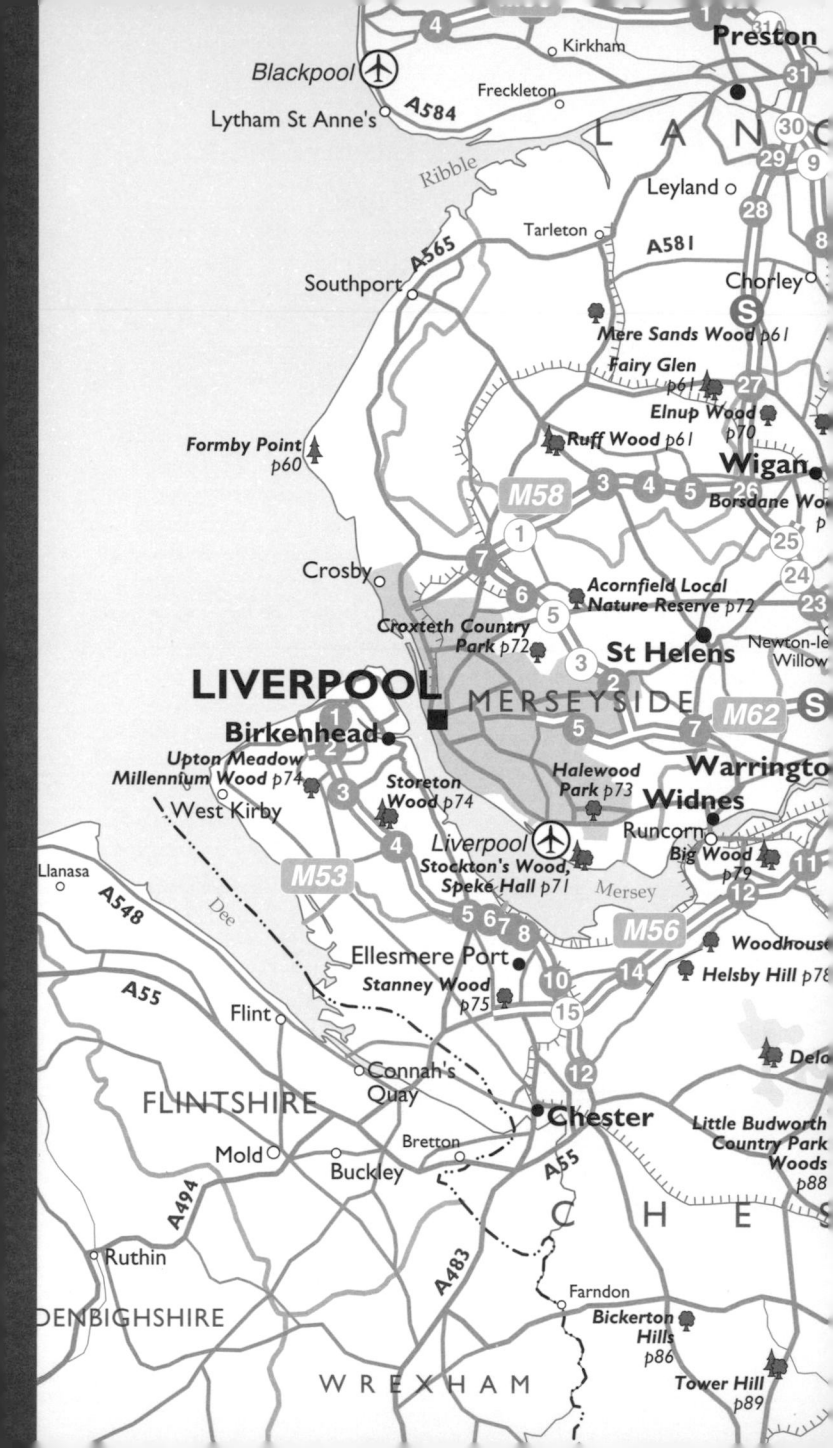

Preston

Kirkham

Blackpool ✈

A584

Freckleton

Lytham St Anne's

L A N C

31A

1

31

30

29 9

Ribble

Leyland o

Tarleton o

A581

28

8

Southport

A565

Chorley o

S

Mere Sands Wood p61

Fairy Glen
p61

27

Elnup Wood
p70

Formby Point
p60

Ruff Wood p61

Wigan

M58

3   4   5

Borsdane Wo
p

26

25

24

Crosby

7

1

Acornfield Local
Nature Reserve p72

23

6

Croxteth Country
Park p72

5

St Helens

Newton-le
Willow

3

LIVERPOOL

M E R S E Y S I D E

M62

S

Birkenhead

1

5

7

Warrington

Upton Meadow
Millennium Wood p74

2

Storeton
Wood p74

Halewood
Park p73

Widnes

West Kirby

3

Liverpool ✈

Runcorn

Big Wood
p79

11

Llanasa

A548

M53

4

Stockton's Wood,
Speke Hall p71

Mersey

12

Dee

5 6 7

8

M56

Woodhouse

A55

Ellesmere Port

Stanney Wood
p75

10

14

Helsby Hill p78

Flint o

15

Connah's
Quay

12

Dela

FLINTSHIRE

Mold o

Bretton

Chester

Little Budworth
Country Park
Woods
p88

Buckley

A55

C   H   E

A494

o Ruthin

A483

DENBIGHSHIRE

Farndon

Bickerton
Hills
p86

W R E X H A M

Tower Hill
p89

Formby Point

Formby
Turn off A565 onto B5424 and follow
brown tourist signs to Formby Point.
(SD275082)
209HA (517ACRES) SSSI
The National Trust

Sand, sea and squirrels are the
ingredients that make a visit to
Formby Point a unique woodland experience. Tall pines,
planted in 1900, tower above
an undulating landscape of old
sand dunes.

Famous for its red squirrels
– descendants of the darker
continental species – these
delightfully bold creatures give
visitors the rare chance of a
close encounter. This is
especially fun for children who
can buy squirrel food from a
National Trust kiosk.

The pines are attractive and
well spaced, contrasting with
denser areas of scrubby
broadleaved woodland of
birch, sycamore, ash, oak and
poplar. Open grassland areas
add to this fascinating
patchwork of habitats. Closer
to the sea, trees give way to
sand dunes with marram grass
and a sandy beach beyond.

Walking is easy thanks to a
network of paths through the
plantation to the sea, some
providing circular walks. It is
usually dry underfoot so walking
boots are rarely needed.

Formby Point

Mere Sands Wood

Ormskirk

Leave A59 in Rufford village along Holmewood Road, B5246. Reserve entrance down drive 1.6km (1 mile) on left. (SD447157)

42HA (104ACRES) SSSI

Wildlife Trust for Lancashire, Manchester & North Merseyside

A woodland oasis in the flat agricultural land of West Lancashire, Mere Sands Wood is packed with interest and activity.

Everyone, from young children to keen naturalists, will find something to please on this reserve which features a mix of habitats including varied woodland, dry heath, grassland and lakes.

The reserve is an important habitat for water voles and supports lots of breeding woodland birds, dragonflies and over-wintering wildfowl.

Oak, rhododendron and beech were planted in the 19th century, but today's visitor will find birch, oak and a small, wartime plantation of Scots pine.

Once a thriving red squirrel population existed here but grey squirrels are now a more common sight. To entice the reds back, spruce and larch have been planted.

Access over this flat site is good, with well-surfaced paths and two waymarked trails. Paths suitable for wheelchair use were extended to 2km in summer 2003.

Ruff Wood

Ormskirk

Turn off A570 at Scarth Hill and then left into Ruff Lane. Ruff Wood approx 200m on left. (SD426075)

8HA (20ACRES)

West Lancs District Council

Fairy Glen

Parbold

Turn off A5209 on to B5375. Turn down Stoneygate Lane. The entrance to Fairy Glen is at the far end of this lane. (SD517106)

10HA (24ACRES)

West Lancs District Council

Lever Park

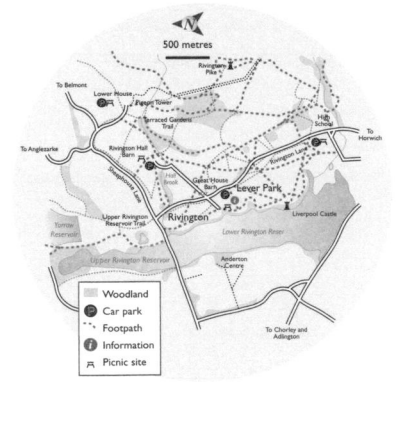

Horwich

Going north on A673 out of Horwich, turn right into Lever Park Avenue and 2km (1.5 miles) to Great House Barn car park. (SD635128)

152HA (376ACRES)

United Utilities

Beautiful woodland, fields and the parkland draws thousands of people to Lever Park but, thanks to the abundance of tree cover, no visitor need ever feel part of a crowd.

The site – a large area of designed landscape – stands within what is now Rivington Country Park and stretches from the Rivington reservoirs and Horwich village over moorland up to Rivington Pike.

Industrial philanthropist Lord Leverhulme, who owned the estate at the turn of the 20th century, had a passion for landscaping which he was able to indulge fully here.

Tree-lined avenues and numerous woodland areas provide a delightful variety of trees from oak, birch and beech to sycamore, horse chestnut and sweet chestnut.

Lord Leverhulme called on the renowned landscape architect Thomas Mawson to help him create impressive hillside gardens around his residence beneath Rivington Pike.

After the war, much of the garden was allowed to become overgrown but recent work by volunteers has reopened paths, allowing some of the most stunning features of the estate to re-emerge.

Today children in particular can enjoy a magical experience, exploring the 'secret' features that lie practically hidden among the woodlands beneath the Pigeon Tower on Rivington Moor, site of Lord Leverhulme's residence.

It is a place where the young can get swept up in make-believe, exploring the maze of terraces and steps and discovering the ponds, falls, follies and lawns that once adorned the windswept hillside.

And while the children indulge their imagination, grown ups can discover the gardens in more detail. A trail leaflet from the Great House information centre provides a plan and descriptions to help visitors explore the gardens and identify the remaining features.

Walker Fold Woodlands

Bolton

Turn off B6226 Chorley Old Road onto Walker Fold Road at Bob's Smithy Inn. Restricted parking is approx 1.6km (1 mile) on the left hand side opposite cottages just before the wood. (SD676124)

18HA (44ACRES)

Bolton MBC

Nestling in the valley of open hill country, Walker Fold Woodland is a contrasting combination of conifer plantations and remnants of the oak woodland that must once have covered the Pennines.

Much of the site is coniferous – Japanese larch and Scots pine planted in the late 1950s – but cover is not dense, with numerous open areas. Well-made, if occasionally muddy, footpaths link with the surrounding hills, creating potential for interesting short walks and lovely country views.

Attractive woodland covers several steep cloughs. Nearby are many areas of recently planted broadleaves – part of a programme which is helping to create the Red Rose Forest.

Wood sorrel growing in patches beneath the conifers contrasts with pink purslane that abounds in the deciduous woodland. Common valerian and common spotted orchid grow sporadically in the nearby field.

Roe deer live in the woodland while long-eared owl populate the surrounding hills and an upland stream running through the wood provides a habitat for grey wagtails.

High Shores Clough Woodland

Bolton

Exit the A58 Bolton ring road at Moss Bank Park traffic lights onto Barrow Bridge Road. The Barrow Bridge car park is approx 1.6km (1 mile) along this road on the left. (SD686118)

17HA (42ACRES)

Bolton MBC

High Shores is typical of the distinctive clough woodlands leading down from the moors.

Compare this with nearby Raveden Wood, another clough woodland which was replanted when it became incorporated into the landscape for Smithills Hall.

While ferns, Himalayan balsam and hogweed line the stream's edge, higher up the valley the ground cover is more typical of moorland and includes bilberry.

A short circular walk, full of variety, climbs up through the woodland and on to the open

moorland. From here lovely views extend across open countryside and is a perfect spot for a picnic. The return route takes you down the 63 steps originally used by miners to reach the mines and quarries on the moors from their village.

The scale of the woodland is ideal for children who will enjoy the small stream and counting the steps. A visit to the Smithill Hall visitor farm could complete a day out for both the young at heart and of mind.

Wilderswood

Horwich, Bolton

Turn off B6266 Chorley Old Road onto Georges Lane. Go straight on for approx 1.6km (1 mile) to car park at main gate to woodland. (SD652125) 9HA (22ACRES)
Bolton MBC

Planted on an exposed hillside during the second half of the last century, Wilderswood packs a lot of interest into a short walk.

The shelter of this plantation woodland, which is fairly dense in parts, contrasts effectively with surrounding open moorland and provides panoramic views over the surrounding countryside which includes the Red Rose Forest. From the western edge you can gaze across Horwich to the coast beyond.

A varied network of well-marked, sometimes muddy paths serves some interesting landmarks, including a disused quarry on the western boundary and the site of an old house. Young beech planted along Old Rake Way above the quarry creates an attractive miniature avenue.

Big Wood (see p79)

Raveden Wood

Raveden Wood, Smithills Hall Estate

Bolton

Turn off A58 Bolton ring road onto
Smithills Dean Road. Approx 800m
(0.5 mile) turn right into Smithills Hall
and car parks. (Also signposted from
A666 going north. Follow sign and then
go straight across at traffic lights at ring
road junction into Smithills Dean
Road.) (SD700120)
19HA (47ACRES)
Bolton MBC

With its blend of ancient
woodland, newer planting and
formal landscaping, Raveden is
a steep clough woodland
which was added to the
Smithills Hall estate in
Victorian times. The rolling
landscape with exposed rock
faces and small streams provide
interest and incident.

At the northern end, a thick
canopy of trees and
understorey of rhododendron
enclose the path which runs
alongside a meandering stream
with waterfall. Further down,
the clough opens into an area
dominated by beech where
dappled sunlight reaches the
woodland floor.

The scenery changes as you
move further down where oak
and sycamore replace beech
with a dense understorey of
young saplings.

A main path loops through
the woodland, leading to
smaller paths and bridges that
cross the stream.

Extend your visit to nearby
High Shores Clough
Woodland (p64) on the edge of
the moors to see a wood of
contrasting character.

Phillips Park 🏞

Whitefield, Manchester
Turn off A665 Higher Lane into Park
Lane. Entrance to park is at end of lane.
(SD796040)
13HA (32ACRES)
Bury MBC

🅿 🏛 🖼

A walk through mixed deciduous
woodland on the hillside of
Phillips Park is an ever changing
experience.

Along the top of the beech,
sycamore, oak and pine
adorned slopes are attractive
walks with open views across
Manchester and the Red Rose
Forest, of which this is a part.
Large hollies are a feature of
this area.

As you descend into the
valley, areas of birch, rowan
and oak give way to poplar,
elm, lime and willow where
hogweed, willowherb, butterbur
and ramson grow along the
damp riverside. At the base of
the valley, the woodland
becomes more enclosed and
sheltered.

Emerge from the woods and
you find yourself in patches of
open grassland. Willowherb,
meadowsweet and common
spotted orchid grow in the
valley meadows while, on
higher ground, more orchids
grow among clumps of willow.

A network of paths creates a
number of circular walks. A
pond, complete with viewing
platform, is worth discovering
in the wood.

Blackley Forest 🏞

Blackley, Manchester
Turn off A576 into Blackley New Road.
Entrance to wood 250m on left. Also
entrance at north end of site from
Victoria Avenue off A576, Middleton
Road. (SD840034)
21HA (52ACRES)
Manchester City Council

🅿 🏛 🖼 ⬚

Jumbles Country Park 🏞

Bolton
Take A676 signposted Ramsbottom.
The A676 takes a sharp right turn at the
Crofter's Arms into Bradshaw Road.
Approx 1.6km (1 mile) on left is
Jumbles Country Park and car park.
(SD737139)
22HA (54ACRES)
United Utilities

🅿 🖼 ⬚ 🚶 ⛺ 📷

Tandle Hill Country Park 🔲

Royton

From A671 through Royton turn into Tandle Hill Road, following signs to country park. Car park at end of this road. (SD906086)

23HA (56ACRES)

Oldham MBC

If you are looking for a unique woodland experience, visit Tandle Hill Country Park.

A hillside site with striking views towards Manchester, the almost exclusively beech wood is something of a rarity in the northwest.

The dense beech canopy arrests any growth on the woodland floor and the wood seems stripped down to basic structural elements. Varied shapes of dark beech trunks are set against a rusty orange layer of leaf litter on an undulating woodland floor with a bright green canopy above, creating an almost sculptural effect.

Known for its toadstools and mushrooms, Tandle Hill also has a fascinating history. The first trees were planted in 1820 to prevent radicals practising marching and drilling following the Peterloo Massacre in Manchester.

Today the experience is a peaceful one. A good network of paths aids access to other areas of Scots pine and larch and some oak regeneration. Picnic tables are provided and wooden sculptures dot the site.

Daisy Nook Country Park 🔲

Ashton-under-Lyne, Oldham

From A627 Ashton Road turn down Newmarket Road and then into Stannybrook Road. Entrance to country park immediately on right. Another car park off A627 approx 1km (0.75 mile) north of Newmarket Road turning. (SD922006)

36HA (89ACRES)

Oldham MBC

River and meadow, lake and woodland can all be found at Daisy Nook Country Park, on the Ashton canal.

Paths lead through a variety of habitats including historic Boodle Wood by the River Medlock where the sound of running water and birdsong add to the wood's peaceful quality.

There are many discoveries to be made in the mixed woodland. Look for planted specimens which remind visitors of the site's former existence as an arboretum for nearby Riversvale Hall, now in ruins. Beech trees once lined the drive and these have now colonised the valley side. From here, views extend across the river and, on sunny days, light catching the tall trunks brings the wood to life.

Flora – typical of riverside woodland – includes hogweed, meadowsweet, ramson, rushes and the invasive Himalayan balsam. Giant-leaved butterbur edges the river. The wood is particularly rich in autumn fungi.

Strinesdale Countryside Area

Oldham
Signposted from A62 Huddersfield Road. Turn into Culvert Street approx 2.5km (1.5 miles) from Oldham town centre. (SD958065)
25HA (62ACRES)
United Utilities

Eastwood

Stalybridge
Take the A6018 (Mottram Road) to Stalybridge and turn off into the car park for Stalybridge Celtic adjacent to the Fox and Hounds public house. Pedestrian entrance next to football ground. (SJ970979)
5HA (12ACRES)
Cheshire Wildlife Trust

Stockton's Wood (see p73)

Elnup

Elnup Wood

Shevington, Nr Wigan
From B5206 turn down Park Brook
Lane. Entrance to wood is on bend at
end of road. (SD552090)
15HA (37ACRES)
Groundwork Wigan & Chorley

To find out how effectively
woodland can transform
industrial wasteland, look no
further than Elnup Wood.

This ancient woodland was
once the site of extensive coal
mining operations yet the steep-
sided valley of Mill Brook
shows little evidence of this
activity. Today it is managed as
a community woodland,
popular with local residents.

There are distinct areas
within this predominantly

broadleaved woodland, each
with its own character. You'll
find oak, birch, ash and hazel
growing higher up the valley
sides, mature beech trees on
the steep slopes and some areas
of younger regeneration.
Below, the sound of Mill
Brook can be heard flowing
gently in a series of small falls
over the sandstone bedrock.

Mining relics, including coal
tanks, can still be found within
the wood but the mounds of
excavated spoil along the valley
floor have been colonised by
sycamore.

Together with three adjoining
woods, totalling more than
34 hectares, these form part of
the Red Rose Forest.

Haigh Hall

Wigan/Aspull
Junction 27 on the M6, A49 to Standish,
followed by B5329 to Haigh, or
junction 6 on the M6, taking B5329 to
Haigh. Haigh can be found between
A49 and A6. (SD598085)
101HA (250ACRES)
Wigan MBC

A tapestry of broadleaved
woodland, the parkland
around Haigh Hall was first
planted more than 100 years
ago. Today it forms part of the
Red Rose Forest and provides

an important 'green corridor' into the town of Wigan.

Here you can enjoy oak, sycamore, birch, rowan, horse chestnut and lime growing alongside attractive areas of beech with some lovely, majestic specimens. The scenery changes constantly, as beech glades alternate with areas of dense woodland and rhododendron-enclosed spaces providing shade and shelter.

More than 40 miles of paths run through the site, including three waymarked trails and a good flat route allowing wheelchairs and buggies to access woodland nearest the hall as well as other parts of the grounds.

Lower down the hillside, separated from the plantations by Yellow Brook, is an ancient woodland known as Bottling Wood which has a completely different character since oak, rather than beech, is the dominant species.

Borsdane Wood

Hindley and Aspull

From Hindley head towards Westhoughton on A58, left into Hindley Mill Lane just before cemetery. Park in lane and walk ahead to unadopted road. Brick tunnel with barrier at front is pedestrian entrance. From Aspull take Bolton Road heading away from Wigan, turn into Mill Lane immediately after Gerrard Arms.

Follow to cobbled road and park in open area then by foot over bridge and through metal squeeze stile. (SD624053) 27HA (67ACRES)
Wigan MBC

Families will love Borsdane Wood. Easy to find your way around, it offers parents peace and tranquillity and provides youngsters a safe and interesting place to explore.

Kind on eye and ear, particularly in spring and summer when alive with birdsong, this ancient woodland feels much larger than it is. The going is easy thanks to a dry, well surfaced path that provides good buggy access. A series of smaller paths lead to footbridges crossing the stream.

You will find a tremendous variety of indigenous and planted species – among them oak, ash, birch, alder, horse chestnut, lime and wild cherry – not to mention sweet chestnut, sycamore, poplars and willow. Occasional groups of beech provide a change of character while ground flora includes bluebell, wild garlic and butterbur.

This linear wood, which sits within the Red Rose Forest, has open farmland to either side with a number of pretty open glades in the southern end which would be perfect for picnics.

Acornfield Local Nature Reserve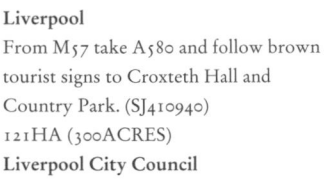

Kirkby

From M57 junction 4 take A580 towards
St Helens and turn left into Coopers
Lane at traffic lights. At roundabout
turn right into Perimeter Road and then
next left into Spinney Road. There is a
small lay-by on right. (SJ437976)
13HA (31ACRES)
Knowsley Borough Council

A cornfield Plantation was
originally planted for game
cover on the basin mire which
once dominated the Kirkby area.
The open bog that remains within
the woodland is a fascinating
remnant of a lost landscape.

A network of grassy rides
and narrow, winding paths lead
through wetland areas with
stands of flag iris, a central
open area of sphagnum bog, a
pond rich with dragonflies and
damselflies, drainage ditches
where water voles have been
spotted and rich areas of
bracken, birch and mixed
deciduous woodland.

Some 70 bird species have
been recorded, including
greater spotted woodpeckers,
jays and owls.

Croxteth Country Park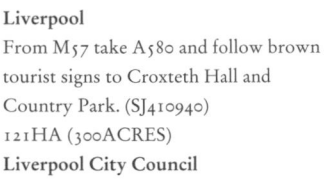

Liverpool

From M57 take A580 and follow brown
tourist signs to Croxteth Hall and
Country Park. (SJ410940)
121HA (300ACRES)
Liverpool City Council

A patchwork of fields and
woodland, the park is rich in
bird species including jays,
nuthatches, blackcap, chiff-chaff
and greater spotted woodpecker.

A good network of paths
provides plenty of opportunities
to explore more remote
corners of the park. Most of
the woods feature typical estate
planting and include ash,

Croxteth Country Park

beech, sycamore, lime, sweet and horse chestnut, Scots and black pine and some impressive oak including the unusual Lucombe oak.

There are replanted areas, rich in ground flora such as bluebells, wood anemones, ramsons, red campion and moschatel. One of the richest is Mull Wood, where access is restricted though there are regular guided walks and a permit system operates. Closer to the Hall is Wilderness Wood, an amenity wood with an attractive walk and a range of ornamental and native species.

Stockton's Wood, Speke Hall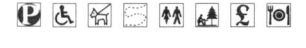

Liverpool

Follow brown tourism signs to Speke Hall. (SJ420825)

57HA (141ACRES) SSSI

The National Trust

This lovely site has a tranquil feel despite the presence of a neighbouring airport!

Dead and dying timber provides a valuable habitat for rare beetles while in spring the woodland floor has a vivid bluebell carpet.

Planted in the 17th century with oak, beech and sweet chestnut to provide timber for the Speke Hall estate, there is a sense of peace in the woodland interior.

Mature spreading trees grow among young birch with bramble and rhododendron beneath – the latter is earmarked for removal. Dense undergrowth encircles more open areas and you can enjoy good views standing beneath the canopy of some lovely mature trees, including gnarled sweet chestnut and some unusual oaks apparently growing on 'stilts'.

Access is via a waymarked trail and some well-surfaced, level paths with wheelchair and buggy access in the southern section.

Halewood Park

Halewood/Liverpool

From junction 6 of the M62 take the A5080 to Huyton. At first set of traffic lights turn left into Whitefield Lane. At the T-junction turn left into Netherley Road and then first right into Greensbridge Lane. Then turn into Cartbridge Lane. Turn right at the T-junction and then straight on at round-about into Okell Drive. Follow the road around and you will see the visitor centre and car park on the left. (SJ442859)

28HA (69ACRES)

Knowsley Borough Council

Upton Meadow Millennium Wood

Wirral, Merseyside
Lies on the northwestern tip of the
Wirral peninsula close to the town of
Birkenhead, between the villages of
Upton and Greasby. (SJ265877)
11HA (27ACRES)
The Woodland Trust

Nestling in an intensely urban
area close to Birkenhead,
Upton Meadow is an oasis for
people and wildlife alike.

It encompasses a network of
ecologically important
habitats. But it is also a vital
recreational resource for local
people, who make good use of
some 1.5 km of footpaths. The
public bridleway along its
western boundary provides an
important link for the people
of Upton and Greasby to
Arrowe Park and beyond.

Well loved and used, the
woodland, a wide and varied
mix of native broadleaves and
shrubs, was created as part of
the Woodland Trust's 'Woods
on Your Doorstep' initiative.

Visitors can explore the
lowland tree mix of Upton
Bridge Wood or enjoy the
grassland on Southern Meadow.
A pond in the north of the site
sustains many invertebrates
and amphibians – including a
healthy toad population.

Arrowe Brook, which
marks the west boundary, is
an excellent wildlife corridor
with a rich mix of plants,
shrubs and trees along its
bank.

Storeton Wood

Higher Bebington
Close to Storeton and Higher
Bebington, entrances via Marsh Lane,
Mount Road and Resthill Road.
(SJ313849)
13HA (31ACRES)
The Woodland Trust

Today Storeton Wood is a
tranquil oasis in an urban
landscape – complete with
butterflies, birds and even
dinosaur footprints!

The fossilised prints are
believed to belong to a
raptor-like dinosaur which
was named after the location,
Cheirotherium storeonia.
They came to light in the
1920s and are now housed in
Liverpool Museum and the
British Museum.

On the site of an old sandstone quarry dating back to
Roman times, the woods are
an attractive landscape
feature in an area of
development pressure. In
fact, Storeton is located in
one of the least wooded parts
of the UK and enjoyed all the

Storeton

Stanney Wood

Little Stanney
A5117 from M53, west of Little
Stanney. Signposted from A5117.
(SJ397738)
9HA (22ACRES)
Ellesmere Port & Neston BC

This remnant of ancient wet woodland was originally part of one of the four crown forests of Cheshire.

Tucked between road and housing, this parcel of land boasts a surprisingly attractive variety of trees including oak, sycamore, birch, hazel, elder and holly. Beneath the tall mature specimens there is a healthy younger generation emerging.

A choice of three waymarked routes, including a 'healthy trail', pass through the wood on level, well-surfaced paths. These are popular with local people who enjoy the pleasant short strolls. A further network of minor paths invites exploration of the quieter parts of the wood.

The site was recognised for its importance to local wildlife by being designated a Local Nature Reserve in 1993.

more by local residents.

Careful and enthusiastic management has created a wildlife haven where butterflies such as the red admiral and small copper and birds such as jay, lesser spotted woodpecker and kestrels thrive. The Woodland Trust receives considerable support from the Friends of Storeton Wood who helped to purchase the wood and still today raise funds and organise workdays to help conserve this valuable woodland.

Delamere Forest

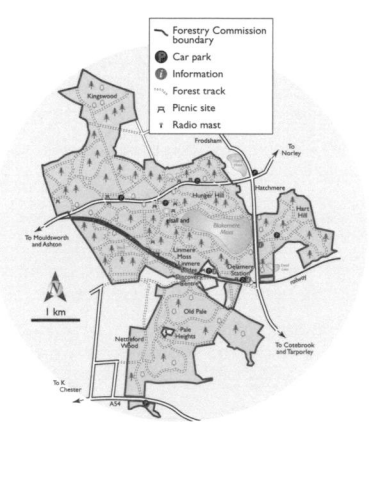

Forestry Commission boundary
P Car park
i Information
Forest track
Picnic site
Radio mast

Kingswood
Frodsham
To Norley
Hunger Hill
Hatchmere
Harts Hill
Linmere Moss
Delamere Station
To Mouldsworth and Ashton
1 km
Old Pale
Nettleford Wood
Pale Heights
To Cotebrook and Tarporley
To K Chester
A54

Northwich and Chester

Turn north off A556 on to B5152, turn left just before Delamere Station, follow road to visitor centre. (SJ547705)
430HA (1,063ACRES) SSSI
Forestry Commission

Cheshire's largest area of woodland, Delamere Forest is a remnant of the ancient forest of Mara and Mondrum and offers some wonderful walks to delight and interest the visitor.

The forest has an interesting background. Once rich in game – red and roe deer and wild boar – it became the exclusive hunting grounds of the Earls of Chester and

protected by Forest Law.

Later the site was exploited for peat, sand and gravel and eventually much of it reverted to heathland. After the World War I it was planted with conifers and today is dominated by Corsican pine though there are some large broadleaved areas with oak and sweet chestnut.

Today this great mix of habitats, including mosses and meres, supports a colourful variety of birds including greater spotted and green woodpeckers, siskins and cross-bills. Delamere is well known for its dragonfly and damselfly populations – no fewer than 15 different species have been recorded.

Thanks to an extensive network of forest rides and paths throughout the site, there is ample opportunity to explore the myriad of habitats tucked among the trees.

Black Lake is a developing 'schwingmoor' – a carpet of sphagnum moss floating over fluid peat and water. Here you might spot unusual plants such as the carnivorous sundew.

Another lake on the site – Hatchmere – is worth seeking out as it offers plenty of opportunity for birdwatching.

A recent development at Delamere is a wetland experiment. The work is focused on a former mire that was originally drained by Napoleonic prisoners who were drafted in after the Battle of Waterloo. Foresters are felling trees and building sluices across drains as part of a project aimed at restoring the site to its natural state.

Helsby Hill

Helsby

Exit 14 off M56, follow A56 toward Helsby. Take right fork (Robin Hood Lane) for 1km (0.75 mile) then left at crossroads. Car park 800m (0.5 mile) on left. (SJ492745)

15HA (37ACRES)

The National Trust

Adorning the approach to a windswept rocky outcrop overlooking the Mersey stands the lovely small woodland of Helsby Hill where rocky sandstone outcrops add drama to the scenery.

Easy walking with short, not-too-difficult climbs takes the visitor up through the woodland of oak, birch, holly and rowan and a ground cover of ferns and bracken, to the summit of Helsby Hill.

Towards the top of the hill the trees have become shaped and stunted by the wind and the wood eventually gives way to bare rock and pockets of heath vegetation.

One path winds up past craggy outcrops and trees and out between tall hedgerows to a field before joining another path that leads back into the wood and out onto the summit – a lovely short walk full of interest.

From here the visitor can take in splendid panoramic views north across the Mersey, west into Wales and to the south and east across the Cheshire countryside.

Helsby Hill

Big Wood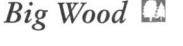

Runcorn

On the northeastern edge of Runcorn adjacent to Norton Priory. (SJ551830)
9HA (23ACRES)
The Woodland Trust

  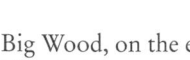

Big Wood, on the edge of the historic Norton Priory site, has a chequered history.

Once part of the Norton manor estate, it passed to the Brookes family following the dissolution of the monasteries in Tudor times. They created woodland walks and pleasure gardens, transforming the site in the mid 18th century.

Dramatic changes continued until 1874 when new paths and vistas were created. However, after the Brookes family left the house in 1921, Big Wood's fortunes suffered. The Runcorn Expressway halved the site and more pressure came from housing development.

Things began to improve in the 1980s when major improvements were made to the footpaths and since then a pond, ditch and woodland restoration programme, including the removal of more than 2 hectares of invasive rhododendron, has been completed.

Today the woodland boasts a good mix of trees and shrubs, including pendunculate and turkey oak, sycamore, alder, silver birch and yew, with a large pond at its heart.

Woodhouse Hill, Snidley Moor and Frodsham Hill Woods

Frodsham

Located 1.6km (1 mile) southwest of Frodsham, Woodhouse Hill adjoins Snidley Moor Wood (SJ513752) in southeast corner. Frodsham Hill Wood (SJ519771) is on the southwest outskirts of Frodsham/Overton and 1km (0.75 mile) NE of Woodhouse Hill Wood. (SJ510754)
54HA (133ACRES)
The Woodland Trust

Owley Wood 🔲

Weaverham

A49 to Weaverham then B5142 and
B5153. Past shopping area, turn left into
Wallerscote Road and left into Owley
Wood Road. (SJ625743)
6HA (15ACRES)
Cheshire Wildlife Trust

Peace, broken only by the
sound of birdsong and the
gentle movement of the River
Weaver, is one of the prime
delights of Owley Wood.

This ancient clough
woodland clothes the steep east-
facing slope of the river valley.

Managed as a community
woodland for almost a decade
and home to a variety of
woodland birds, this is a
broadleaved wood of sycamore,
ash and alder with a rich
understorey of hazel, hawthorn,
holly, elder and goat willow.

Adding to the character of
the wood are some lovely
mature oak and sweet chestnut
trees. Small streams flowing
down the slope feed into a
river where ducks and swans
can often be seen swimming.

Well-surfaced paths and
boardwalk sections provide
a circular walk along the
riverside and up the slope to
the top of the wood for a
lovely view overlooking the
river and valley.

Marbury Country Park 🔲

Comberbach/Northwich

1.6km (1 mile) north of Northwich,
entrance off Comberbach/Barnton
road. From A559 follow brown tourist
signs to country park. (SJ654762)
86HA (213ACRES)
Cheshire County Council

If you are looking for a walk
full of interest and variety,
make a visit to Marbury
Country Park.

Marbury Hall is long gone
but the parkland of the old
estate remains and the
woodlands that fringe the park
provide gentle but feature-
filled walks along well-surfaced
paths through woods of
contrasting character.

Big Wood, which lies along
the southern shore of
Budworth Mere, has occasional
clearings amongst oak, ash,
sycamore and chestnut plus
small ponds and a hide to
watch woodland birds such as
chiff-chaff and willow warbler.
Bluebells and wood anemones
provide a fine spring show.

Further along, the wood runs
parallel with the Cheshire Ring
Canal and the mood changes
with birch and Scots pine taking
centre stage. The path continues
into Hopyard Wood, a broadleaved
area within the valley of the

gently meandering Cogshall Brook. Here the understorey is denser and the wood darker and more enclosed.

Park Moss

Arley, Warrington
From Appleton take Arley Road south. Cross over the M56 and follow road for about 3km (2 miles). Woodland entrance on left. (SJ660817)
10HA (24ACRES)
The Woodland Trust

Park Moss Wood is located to the south of Warrington and near the village of Arley.

When acquired by the Woodland Trust in 1985 a section of Corsican pine was cleared to make way for a mix of broadleaves to be planted. Visit this section to see a wood in the making.

The slim white trunks of silver birch predominate with oak, Scots pine, willow, holly, alder, wild cherry and buckthorn among the trees to be found here. Distinctive fronds of different varieties of fern texture the woodland floor in a variety of lush greens.

As the wood's name implies, the site lies on a peaty, low lying remnant of mossland. A series of open ditches surround the wood to aid drainage.

Access is good – the site contains two public rights of way – although visitors in winter are advised that the ground can become wet.

Park Moss Wood

Lumb Brook Valley

Warrington
Lies in the Appleton area of south
Warrington. Park on Dingle Lane.
(SJ627849)
9HA (22ACRES)
The Woodland Trust

You get four woods for the
price of one as Lumb Brook
Valley is in reality a collection
of interconnected but
distinctive woodland sites.

The Fords Rough contains
an area of ancient woodland
while, in the valley, you will
discover a diverse range of
shrubs and flowers. A surfaced,
if sometimes waterlogged,
footpath provides access
through the length of the wood.

The Dingle is a large wooded
valley offering a variety of
broadleaf and conifers. A well-
used footpath meanders through
sparse ground vegetation but
pockets of colourful flowers
emerge here each spring. The
site is under pressure from
development but was extended
by the Woodland Trust in 1998
to buffer the woodland from
the impact of farming on one
side and housing on the other.

By contrast, Long Wood has
many maturing oaks with
dense layers of rhododendron
beneath.

Add nearby 17-acre
Grappenhall Heys and 20-acre
Grappenhall Wood to your
visit and you could explore six
woods in one day.

Lumb Brook Valley

Grappenhall Heys

Warrington
To the south of Warrington where new
roads have been built to service new
housing development. Grappenhall
Heys can be accessed via Astor Drive.
Go through ornate wrought iron gates
on right and follow surfaced track.
(SJ630856)
7HA (17ACRES)
The Woodland Trust

Grappenhall Wood

Warrington
Off Broad Lane, Grappenhall,
Warrington. Follow public footpath
waymarker signs via Australia Lane.
(SJ641858)
8HA (20ACRES)
The Woodland Trust

Risley Moss

Warrington
M62, junction 11, follow A574 over
three roundabouts following signs to
Risley Moss. (SJ663921)
10HA (25ACRES) SSSI
Warrington Borough Council

In this rare surviving fragment
of the boggy wasteland that
once dotted the Mersey Valley
lie the woodlands of Risley Moss.

You will discover a pleasant
mosaic of dense birch and
sunny clearings – many sculptures too – with seats and
benches located at regular
intervals along well-surfaced
woodland paths.

Peat was harvested from the
Moss in the 1800s and, during
World War II, a munitions
factory occupied part of the
site. After the war it became
derelict and wildlife reclaimed
once again.

A hide and observation
tower provide vantage points
to view barn owls, hobbies,
hen harriers and other wildlife.
Public access to the Moss itself
is restricted to guided walks.

Gorse Covert Mounds

Warrington
Car park off Gorse Covert Road,
Birchwood, Warrington. (SJ665928)
17HA (42ACRES)
The Woodland Trust

Spud Wood

Oughtrington
Between Oughtrington Lane in the west
and Burford Lane to the east. (SJ701871)
17HA (42ACRES)
The Woodland Trust

Alderley Edge

Alderley Edge

From Alderley Edge village take B5087
Macclesfield Road. Car park 1.6km (1 mile)
on left after Wizard Inn. (SJ860775)
120HA (297ACRES) SSSI
The National Trust

Magical Alderley Edge is the
stuff of myth and legend – no
wonder people love it.

There is a special atmosphere
on this site with its medieval
earthworks, England's oldest
copper mines, beacon and
legend-shrouded Wizard's Well
that draws the crowds,
especially at weekends.

Visit during the week or in
the early morning and evening if
you want to freely explore. The
site's rich history and legends
form an important part of local
folklore and inspired Alan
Garner's popular book 'The
Weirdstone of Brisingamen'.

It is a delightful place to walk
with so much to discover that it
is possible to return many times
and still find something new.
Children love the woods with
sandstone cliffs, caves and mine
entrances or hunting for the Well.

An extensive network of
paths leads to Stormy Point –
where visitors throng to enjoy
wonderful views of the
surrounding countryside.

Styal Estate

Styal

From A57 take Manchester Airport
exit. Follow signs to Quarry Bank Mill.
Signs from Wilmslow. (SJ836829)
50HA (124ACRES)
The National Trust

Adorning a deep valley, carved
by the River Bollin through
sandstone bedrock, the
meandering broadleaved
woodland of the Styal Estate is
a haven for a variety of wildlife.

Fungi adorn the ancient trees
in which woodpeckers thrive
while bluebells carpet the
woodland floor in spring.

The estate incorporates
Quarry Bank Mill, an
apprentice house, mill workers'
village and 300 acres of countryside in the Bollin Valley.

Mainly broadleaves,
complemented by planted
beech, hornbeam, Scots pine and
exotics such as wellingtonia, the
woods have many impressive
mature specimens.

Walking through the southern
section is easy on dry, level and
sandy paths. From the mill to
Tweenies bridge is suitable for
wheelchairs and buggies. The
going gets harder in the steeper
northern woods where boots
are a must.

Macclesfield Forest

Macclesfield
A523 south from Macclesfield, turn left toward Langley, through village then right beside reservoir and first left up towards the ranger centre and main car park. (SJ961714)
400HA (989ACRES)
United Utilities

There is magic in Macclesfield Forest, a large conifer-dominated woodland set around three reservoirs on the slopes of the Peak District hills overlooking the Cheshire Plain.

The most extensive area of broadleaf trees can be found in Brick Kiln Wood, high on the hill above the Trentabank reservoir, where beautiful mature sycamores cling to the side of the hill.

Visitors are well provided for in the forest, with the felling of conifers to make way for native broadleaves and the creation of an excellent network of well-surfaced paths.

As a result, there is a choice of routes, from low-level ambles near the reservoirs with their resident wildfowl to more challenging walks through dense conifer plantations out onto the open moorland above and a wonderful vantage point from the summit of Sutlingsloe, Cheshire's second highest point.

Many woodland birds thrive in the plantation and one stand of tall trees supports Cheshire's largest heronry – a handy viewpoint is provided nearby.

Macclesfield Forest

Bickerton Hills

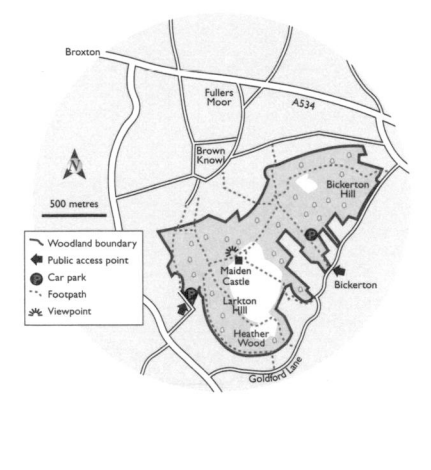

Broxton

Fullers
Moor

A534

Brown
Knowl

Bickerton
Hill

Maiden
Castle

Larkton
Hill

Bickerton

Heather
Wood

Goldford Lane

500 metres

- ⌐ Woodland boundary
- ◄ Public access point
- Ⓟ Car park
- ⋯ Footpath
- ✳ Viewpoint

Bickerton
A534 to Bickerton then right at church.
After 1km (0.75 mile) turn right into
Pool Lane car park. (SJ 505530)
28HA (69ACRES) SSSI
The National Trust

On a sandstone ridge rising out
of the Cheshire Plain are the
hills of Bickerton, Bulkeley
and Peckforton – three
broadleaved woodlands offering
a great day out.

Bickerton Hill woods are
mainly birch with oak, rowan
and holly, encircling open
heath vegetation of gorse,
bracken and heather on the
summit.

A gentle climb leads to the summit. An Iron Age hillfort – Maiden Castle – stands on the wild but peaceful ridge which boasts panoramic views – a gentle contrast with the distant hum of life on the Cheshire Plain. The remains of earth banks that protected the huts inside are still visible. From here buzzards may be seen circling, their distinctive mewing call a familiar sound at certain times of the year.

Other wildlife to look out for includes the green hairstreak butterfly which feeds on bilberries during the summer. The woodland supports many birds and flocks of tits are common in autumn and winter.

A walk through the nearby oak woods of Bulkeley Hill, also owned by the National Trust, is equally inspiring.

The path leads to a summit scattered with huge sweet chestnuts where views extend to the Peak District, Cannock Chase and the Wrekin. To reach the wood turn off the A534 at Bulkeley toward Peckforton, access at the junction of Stonehouse Lane and Mill Lane.

Public access to the estate woodland of Peckforton Hills may not be as open but there is a good network of paths. Before entering the woodland, via the entrance to Peckforton Castle, take special note of the Wesley oak opposite – one of the oldest trees in Cheshire and named after John Wesley who was said to have preached beneath it in 1749. Keep your eye out for birdlife which includes pied flycatcher and crossbill.

Heaton Park 🖼️

Prestwich, Manchester
Entrances signposted from Old Bury
Road (A665) and Sheepfoot Lane
(A6044). (SD830044)
259HA (640ACRES)
Manchester City Council

[icons]

There is a special, open countryside feel about Heaton Park
that makes it easy to forget the
surrounding busy city.

One of the largest parks in
Europe, it has an array of
attractions including
playgrounds and a farm, set on
a gently rolling landscape criss-
crossed with streams and
ponds. An extensive network
of paths leads through swathes
of woodland areas to contrasting open grassland where
Highland cattle graze.

Located within the Red Rose
Forest, scattered birch trees
dot the grassland, lending an
attractive parkland feel. In contrast, more cultivated gardens
are set around the hall and farm.

Move into the woods and
there is another change of mood
with a varied blend of oak, beech,
sycamore and horse chestnut
ranging from open sections
that invite exploration, to wilder
parts with a dense understorey.
The countryside atmosphere is
particularly marked in Hazlitt
and Stennar Woods.

Brereton Heath Country Park 🅿️

Holmes Chapel/Congleton
A54 from Holmes Chapel. After 2.5km
(1.5 miles) turn right into Davenport
Lane, entrance 450m on left. Site is
signposted. (SJ800650)
34HA (84ACRES)
Cheshire County Council

[icons]

Little Budworth Country Park Woods 🅿️

Little Budworth
At junction of A49/A54 follow sign for
Little Budworth, main car park on left
in southeast corner of site. (SJ587657)
33HA (82ACRES) SSSI
Cheshire County Council

[icons]

Five miles from Delamere
Forest lies Little Budworth
Country Park Woods, a woodland remnant of the evocatively
named ancient hunting forest
of Mara and Mondrum.

Much of the sandy heathland
site is covered with birch
woodland plus oak, holly and
beech. Sunny open clearings
and small areas of open water
add to the interest of this
varied site.

The flowers – mainly gorse
and heather – are typical of
heathland, as are many of the
wildlife species, including

Alderley Edge (see p84)

woodcock and green hairstreak butterfly.

Exploration of this attractive site makes for some easy walking, thanks to the level paths and the woodland floor is generally open with scattered ferns.

Although the woods are dense in places, with light filtering through the birch-dominated canopy to cast a dappled shade on the woodland floor, it never feels oppressive.

Tower Hill

Malpas

Turn west at Cholmondeley Arms crossroads on A49, entrance to Cholmondeley Castle 200m on right. Woodland within grounds of castle.
(SJ549506)
8HA (20ACRES)
The Marquess of Cholmondeley

Recommend a Wood

You can play a part in helping us complete this series. We are inviting readers to nominate a wood or woods they think should be included. We are interested in any woodland with public access in England, Scotland, Wales and Northern Ireland.

To recommend a wood please photocopy this page and provide as much of the following information as possible:

ABOUT THE WOOD:

Name of wood:

Nearest town:

Approximate size:

Owner/manager:

A few words on why you think it should be included:

ABOUT YOU

Your name:

Your postal address:

Post code:

If you are a member of the Woodland Trust please provide your membership number

Please send to: Exploring Woodland Guides, The Woodland Trust, Autumn Park, Dysart Road, Grantham, Lincolnshire NG31 6LL, by fax on 01476 590808 or email woodlandguides@woodland-trust.org.uk

Thank you for your help

Other Guides in the Series

If you would like to be notified when certain titles are due for publication please either write to Exploring Woodland Guides, The Woodland Trust, Autumn Park, Dysart Road, Grantham, Lincolnshire NG31 6LL or email woodlandguides@woodland-trust.org.uk

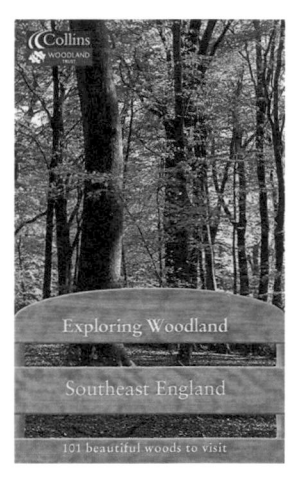

The Woodland Trust

Registered Charity No 294344. The Woodland Trust logo is a registered trademark.

Trees and forests are crucial to life on our planet. They generate oxygen, play host to a spectacular variety of wildlife and provide us with raw materials and shelter. They offer us tranquillity, inspire us and refresh our souls.

Founded in 1972, the Woodland Trust is now the UK's leading woodland conservation charity. By acquiring sites and campaigning for woodland it aims to conserve, restore and re-establish native woodland to its former glory. The Trust now owns and cares for over 1,100 woods throughout the UK. The Woodland Trust wants to see:

* no further loss of ancient woodland
* the variety of woodland wildlife restored and improved
* an increase in new native woodland
* an increase in people's awareness and enjoyment of woodland

The Woodland Trust has over 120,000 members who share this vision. It only costs £2.50 a month to join but your support would be of great help in ensuring the survival of Britain's magnificent woodland heritage. For every new member, the Trust can care for approximately half an acre of native woodland. For details of how to join the Woodland Trust please either ring FREEPHONE 0800 026 9650 or visit the website at www.woodland-trust.org.uk

If you have enjoyed the woods in this book please consider leaving a legacy to the Woodland Trust. Legacies of all sizes play an invaluable role in helping the Trust to create new woodland and secure precious ancient woodland threatened by development and destruction. For further information please either call 01476 581129 or visit our dedicated website at www.legacies.org.uk

Volunteering opportunities

Would you like to help us, protect, improve and expand our precious woods? We are on the look out for new committed volunteers with a range of skills. Our volunteers do a huge range of things.

At the Woodland Trust, we value the donation of time as much as we do the donation of funds. Any work you do for us, whether it is in the woods or in the office will contribute to the Trust's key objectives. To find out more either visit our website or write, fax, give us a call or send an email.

Thank you for supporting our work.

Further Information

Public transport

Each entry gives a brief description of location, nearest town and grid reference. Traveline provides impartial journey planning information about all public transport services either by ringing 0870 608 2608 (calls charged at national rates) or visit www.traveline.org.uk. For information about the Sustrans National Cycle Network either ring 0117 929 0888 or visit www.sustrans.org.uk

Useful contacts

Forestry Commission:
www.forestry.gov.uk
tel: 0845 367 3787

National Trust:
www.nationaltrust.org.uk
tel: 0870 458 4000

Wildlife Trusts:
www.wildlifetrusts.org
tel: 0870 036 7711

RSPB:
www.rspb.org.uk
tel: 01767 680551

Royal Forestry Society:
www.rfs.org.uk
tel: 01442 822028

National Community Forest Partnership:
www.communityforest.org.uk
tel: 01684 311880

Woodland Trust:
www.woodland-trust.org.uk
tel: 01476 581111

Index

Legal & General

Legal & General is delighted to support the Woodland Trust's conservation programme across the UK.

As a leading UK company, Legal & General recognises the importance of maintaining and improving our environment for future generations. We actively demonstrate our commitment through good management and support of environmental initiatives and organisations, such as the Woodland Trust.

Information on how Legal & General manages its impact on the environment can be found at www.legalandgeneral.com/csr.